1622-1673 Jean Baptiste Paquelin, Time of Louis XIV
greatest French writer of comedy. Comic contrast of how people see
themselves and how others see t

Tartuffe - satire on religious hypocrisy
Misanthrope - satirized universal human
Miser
The School for Wives - best?

Harpagon - father

Cleante - son of H

Elise - daughter of H

Valere - servant (noble) & secret lover of Elise

La Fleche - Cleante's servant

Frosine - ♀ matchmaker

La Fl
Master Simon - broker for Cleante & H.

Master Jacques - livery servant of H.

Marianne - beautiful but poor love interest of H. & son

Euselme - Napolian Count, father of V & M

Photo by Ralph Funicello

A set of the South Coast Repertory production of "The Miser." Set design by Ralph Funicello.

THE MISER

BY
MOLIÈRE

TRANSLATED BY
DAVID CHAMBERS

★

★

DRAMATISTS
PLAY SERVICE
INC.

THE MISER
Copyright © 1993, David Chambers

All Rights Reserved

SPECIAL NOTE

THE MISER was first produced by South Coast Repertory (David Emmes, Producing Artistic Director; Martin Benson, Artistic Director), in Costa Mesa, California, on January 8, 1993. It was directed by David Chambers; the set design was by Ralph Funicello; the costume design was by Shigeru Yaji; the lighting design was by Chris Parry; the assistant director was Tim Vasen; the production manager was Ed Lapine and the stage manager was Julie Haber. The cast was as follows:

VALERE ....Jeffrey Combs
ELISE ....Terres Unsoeld
CLEANTE...Reg E. Cathey
HARPAGON...Jonathan McMurtry
LA FLECHE...Don Took
MASTER SIMON*...Art Koustik
FROSINE...Jane Galloway
MASTER JACQUES ....Ron Boussom
MARIANNE...Lynnda Ferguson
CHIEF OF POLICE ....John Ellington
ANSELME...Hal Landon, Jr.

* MASTER SIMON can double with either the CHIEF OF POLICE or ANSELME.

SETTING

Paris, Harpagon's house

TIME

Mid-19th century

TRANSLATOR'S NOTES

Like many contemporary translations, this *Miser* was born of a specific production, in this case at South Coast Repertory in Costa Mesa, California. Unlike many contemporary translations, it was undertaken by one whose trade is that of a director, not a translator. Its roots are in the stage, not the academy; its branches were pruned by actors at work, not editors. Sometimes it is slavishly faithful to the original, other times it revels in verbal improvisation. It is meant to be actor/audience gratifying, and cares little for scholarly rewards. But whatever it is, it remains a translation, not an adaptation.

Throughout the rehearsal process at South Coast Repertory a well-smudged "literal" was consulted, argued over, and thought of as a (fallible) arbiter. Occasionally Jean-Baptiste Moliere's ghost would waft through the rehearsal room to enlighten or chastise us. Sometimes He would roll his eyes but leave us to our twentieth-century American devices. Now and again He would laugh out loud with us. Or at us. More often, He just wouldn't show up, leaving us to guess our way down some slippery slope. But it was His play we were doing, not ours, and no matter what liberty we did or did not take, we were always trying to please our ever-theatrical fellow traveller, Jean-Baptiste.

We left the production in Paris (albeit a 19th-century version). We whittled relentlessly at the language, striving for a lean and rapid actor-based rhythm (this is a primary goal of the translation). We made the now-common excision of several minor characters. We added some "shtick" notably a walking suit of armor, some fourth-wall violation, and a few anachronistic sound cues which we realized future productions might want to dispense with. We re-wrote up to opening night, our final collaborators being the preview audiences who demanded yet more cuts, clarifications, and timing adjustments. Jean-Baptiste almost invariably agreed with His admiring public. What could we do but make the changes?

Future productions of this translation will hopefully try to find that same balance of literary veracity and real-world production vitality that we strove for. The words on these pages are not springboards for free-form paraphrase; they are a text in which every syllable was tested at one point or another. They seek rigorous clarity, rhythm, and performance energy. But on the other hand they are an effort to capture an indefinable internal "spirit" and thus require abandon, imagination, even reckless play, to make them work. Sometimes in rehearsal you will get hung up, as we did, between the rigor and the recklessness and wonder which way to turn.

Call Jean-Baptiste; He knows what He's doing.

THE MISER

ACT ONE

The conservatory/atrium of a once magnificent Parisian townhouse. Decay has set in full-force: windows are broken and stuffed with rags, statuary has been removed from pedestals, an old rug lies rolled in the corner. The few remaining items in the room, a tarnished suit of armor, cracked urns, etc. are marked with price tags. Upstage center are glass doors leading to an equally neglected garden; dead topiary and overgrown weeds abound.

As lights rise we hear 19th-century romantic music, mixed with wind, human moans, and long-suffering music such as Piaf's Je ne regrette rien, *the last of which takes over. The garden doors fly open and clothes sail into the room: a women's frock, a man's boot, a woman's slip, a man's pants. Suddenly dogs in the garden are barking feverishly. A half-clad young woman dashes into the room, pursued by a lesser clad young man.*

VALERE.   Elise, wait! *(She is sobbing.)* Ma cherie, what are these cries? *(She cries.)* Rapture? *(She moans.)* Sorrow? *(She howls.)* Oh God, regret. This is regret! And right in the middle of my ecstasy. You're not backing out on our engagement, are you Elise?

ELISE.   Je ne regrette rien, Valere, rien. But this is dangerous. We're playing with fire. I shake, I quiver.

VALERE.   And I love! You! What could you possibly fear, Elise, when you have me to protect you?

ELISE.   A hundred things: start with my father's rage for one. And if that's not enough, there's my family, my reputation, my honor. Not to mention you; you're a man, Valere; you'll say anything to get what you want. How can I know I can trust you?

VALERE.   We're a bad gender, Elise, I agree. But you must see me as an exception. *My* love is deeper than the ocean, wider than the sea, longer than life, larger than all Paris.

ELISE.   Words, Valere, just words. Promises are one thing, deeds another.

VALERE.   Then open your heart and let my deeds erupt in your soul. See me for what I am, not what you fear me to be. Time, time, time, give me time. A thousand proofs of my love shall be yours.

ELISE.   Oh, I'm such a pushover. One sweet nothing from you and I'm creme brulee. I don't doubt your love, Valere, or your constancy. It's the disapproval of others. Imagine a lifetime of reproachful eyes staring at you.

VALERE.   Why would that bother you?

ELISE.   If only others could see you as I do. Every waking moment, I recall how you pulled me out of the waves on that terrible day, laid me out on the shore and filled me with the breath of life. And now you stay here with me, forced into this hideous masquerade acting as my father's steward, despite your noble upbringing and your long-lost family. All of this has a marvelous effect on me, Valere; I bask in your radiance. But others don't see it that way. They think of you as a ... servant!

VALERE.   Call me whatever they may, it is my passion for you that defines who I truly am: your lover, your protector, your servant. And if that monstrosity of a father of yours, that hideous, avaricious, greedy ogre whose every action threatens to destroy even his own fragile children can't see me for who I am, then, by God I'll travel the globe 'til I find my real family and stand them in front of him. Then the little rodent will see what's what and who's who. Elise, have I gone too far?

ELISE.   Don't leave me, Valere! Not alone with him! I beg you, stay, and try to gain my father's full confidence.

VALERE.   What more can I do? Daily I bow to him, praise

him, offer sympathy, all to win him over. And it's working. He believes me! But what a price: I don't believe a word I say anymore. But on I go praising his voluminous virtues, cackling at his rapier-sharp witticisms and flattering his every whim. And flattery wins every round, Elise, even with the most suspicious. Season a vicious insult with a pinch of praise and the game is won. Meanwhile, I'm on the verge of spontaneous combustion.

ELISE.   Maybe we need to enlist my brother, in case the scullery maid should betray our secret.

VALERE.   Oh, no; one is enough; managing both your father and your brother would be like trying to stop marbles from rolling down a hill. Those two are so at each other's throats, that getting in the middle I'm bound to be pressed into a stain on the carpet. But you, Elise, you have your brother's confidence. You work on him. Now's your chance; he's coming. Me, I'm going. I love you. Do your best, but wait for the right moment. *(He exits. Cleante enters.)*

CLEANTE.   Sister, thank God you're alone! I can't hold it in any longer — You're the only one I can tell!

ELISE.   Tell what, brother?

CLEANTE.   I am in love.

ELISE.   You are in love?

CLEANTE.   I am in love. I am in love. But before you go on, let me assure you that I KNOW that I am my father's son and therefore completely dependent upon his will; I KNOW I owe him my very life; I KNOW that without his consent, fortified by his experience and wisdom, my passions are but mere infantile folly. I KNOW that he is the captain of my destiny and that without him my boat is very small and rudderless, adrift in an ocean of turbulent waves that only his mighty hand can calm. I KNOW THIS! So don't tell it to me, please. It won't work.

ELISE.   Are you engaged yet?

CLEANTE.   That's coming. Soon, very soon. And don't you dare try to dissuade me. It won't work.

ELISE.   Brother Cleante, why would I try to change your mind?

CLEANTE.   From sheer innocence, Elise. Ignorant sweet-
heart, divine innocent, what could you possibly know about
the fiery steel of passion, the honeyed milk of intimacy? One
day the temple of desire will open its throbbing gates and
reveal its inner secrets to you as it has to me.
ELISE.   If only you knew.
CLEANTE.   Knew what?
ELISE.   Knew who it is you love. If only I knew.
CLEANTE.   Ah, Elise; if only you did know. She's new to
this district, and has been locked up tending to her ailing
mother. So you wouldn't have seen her. But if you could,
Elise! She's a triumph of nature, the consummation of God's
handiwork, the brightest star of the firmament. I'm gone,
Elise. Over the waterfall without a paddle.
ELISE.   So I see, brother. But does she have a name?
CLEANTE.   They're poor, Elise. Clean, but very poor. Oh,
sister, imagine the joy of being able to drag her out of the
mire of paucity into a world of plenty; to bestow on her, ever
so delicately, the commodious pleasures of this life — silks,
perfumes, combs, mirrors, and dainties — little tiny, pink
dainties.
ELISE.   Brother! Her name.
CLEANTE.   But here we are stuck with this hideous father
whose avarice cripples us. The scoundrel! He robs me of my
life, my pleasure, my love. He is a basilisk unto my heart.
ELISE.   You do seem perturbed.
CLEANTE.   Just what good will it do us, Elise, to inherit every sous he has hoarded, every article he has hidden or
locked up, when we are too old to frolic in the fields of
youth? Just what do you think it feels like to go about running up debts, putting the tailor off for one more month,
ducking down alleyways to avoid my fellow card-players? What
do you think it feels like, huh! That's why I've come to you,
to enlist you in my cause: I'm going to stand up to him
and get what I need for once; if he doesn't grant me permission to marry, and money, lots of it, then I'm running off
with her anyway.
ELISE.   Who? Name.

CLEANTE.　　And you're coming with me. You, me, and Marianne! We'll take our chances, it'll be risky, but it will be worth it to emancipate ourselves from the tyranny of the oppressor. Sic Semper Tyrannus.

ELISE.　　*(Aside.)* If only mother hadn't died. *(A fuss is heard down the hall.)*

CLEANTE.　　That's him! Quick, let's go plot our strategy. *(As they hide, La Fleche races on pursued by Harpagon.)*

HARPAGON.　　Out, out, out! Out of my house, you cheat, you parasite, you scabie, you repulsive freeloader. Out!

LA FLECHE.　　*(Aside.)* I hate this man! The devil himself feasts on his soul.

HARPAGON.　　What are you muttering about?

LA FLECHE.　　Why are you chasing me? What have I done?

HARPAGON.　　Me? Answer a yelping cur, a slathering mongrel? Ha! Now, out!

LA FLECHE.　　Sir, I am your son's servant, not yours; I wait only on him.

HARPAGON.　　Then go wait for him in the gutter where you both belong. I won't have your prying eyes peering around every corner of this house, snooping about in closets and cupboards sniffing out things to steal. From ME! Snipe. Ferret.

LA FLECHE.　　Steal? From you? You who locks up everything he has and stands sentry by it with his dogs day and night?

HARPAGON.　　*(Aside.)* I'm in a sweat lest this warthog should root out my precious money. You! Take my advice: keep your trap shut about me having money hidden in this house.

LA FLECHE.　　You have money hidden?

HARPAGON.　　I didn't say that.

LA FLECHE.　　You didn't?

HARPAGON.　　You didn't hear that.

LA FLECHE.　　I didn't?

HARPAGON.　　But I wouldn't put it past you to bandy it all over town. Gossip. Rumormonger. Out, out, out!

LA FLECHE.　　Very well, I'm going.

HARPAGON.　　Not so fast. What are you taking with you?

LA FLECHE.　　What could I possibly steal from you?

HARPAGON.　　I don't know 'til I look. Show me your hands.

LA FLECHE. Here they are.

HARPAGON. Now the others.

LA FLECHE. The others?

HARPAGON. The others.

LA FLECHE. Here they are.

HARPAGON. *(Pointing to his breeches.)* What have you got in there?

LA FLECHE. Take a look. *(Pulling out his pockets.)* Did you ever kiss a rabbit on the nose?

HARPAGON. Only a thief like you would wear breeches like those. *(He searches.)*

LA FLECHE. *(Aside.)* Oh, the pleasure it would give me to rob this man blind.

HARPAGON. What's that?

LA FLECHE. What?

HARPAGON. What was that about robbing?

LA FLECHE. Rubbing. I was saying it would give you pleasure to rub me blind to make sure I couldn't steal anything.

HARPAGON. That's what I plan to do.

LA FLECHE. *(Aside.)* May the plague fall on all misers and cheapskates.

HARPAGON. What's that?

LA FLECHE. What?

HARPAGON. What's that about misers and cheapskates?

LA FLECHE. May the yellow fog of pestilence rain on them.

HARPAGON. Who's them?

LA FLECHE. Misers and cheapskates.

HARPAGON. Anyone in particular?

LA FLECHE. All misers and cheapskates.

HARPAGON. Such as?

LA FLECHE. Such as who?

HARPAGON. Such as who do you mean?

LA FLECHE. What do you think I mean?

HARPAGON. I think what I think. But what do you think?

LA FLECHE. About what?

HARPAGON. About who you were addressing.

LA FLECHE. I was addressing myself. I was addressing myself to my cap. Would you prevent me from addressing myself to my cap?

HARPAGON.   I'll prevent you from addressing anyone in insolent, vengeful tones.

LA FLECHE.   If the hat fits, wear it.

HARPAGON.   Enough! Hold your tongue.

LA FLECHE.   Tongue held. *(Showing him an inner pocket.)* Wait! Seems like you overlooked one.

HARPAGON.   Out with it.

LA FLECHE.   Out with what?

HARPAGON What you've stolen from me.

LA FLECHE.   I've stolen nothing from you.

HARPAGON.   Have!

LA FLECHE.   Haven't!

HARPAGON.   Get the hell out of my house. *(He is alone.)* Oh the horror, the horror! Keeping a large sum of money hidden inside your house — see what it does, see what it does! Every creak of the floor, every chirp of a bird, every cry from the scullery and I break out in cascades of sweat. But where else to put it? A bank? Hah! Suppose those starch-collared crooks overextended their loans, who would bail them out, the government? Dream on! A safe behind a mirror? The first place any self-respecting burglar would look. I keep my pet viper in there. Oh, how smart I thought I was yesterday when I buried my newly-earned ten thousand crowns in a strongbox in the garden. And chained the Dobermans to the nearest tree. But what if they dig it up and give it to my children? What if the earth erupts and belches forth fire, smelting my coins into a sulfurous river that flows to the Seine? What if ... *(He hears voices.)* Oh Lord, I've been overheard! *(He slaps himself sharply across the cheek.)* Calm, Harpagon, be calm. *(Cleante and Elise enter.)*

CLEANTE.   Father! What are these red stripes across your cheek?

HARPAGON.   Nothing. Nothing at all. Have you been there long?

ELISE.   We were just coming in.

HARPAGON.   You heard.

CLEANTE.   Heard what, father?

13

HARPAGON.   I know it. I know you did.

ELISE.   Know what?

HARPAGON.   You did, you did, you did. I know you did.

CLEANTE.   Did what, father?

HARPAGON.   Heard what I said just now. That's what you did.

ELISE.   We did?

HARPAGON.   I know you did.

CLEANTE.   No! We didn't.

HARPAGON.   Yes, you did!

ELISE.   But, sir ...

HARPAGON.   I was just saying how happy we would all be, particularly me, if only I had ten thousand crowns. Here. In the house. Somewhere. Not anywhere special, just somewhere. If only.

CLEANTE.   Father, Elise and I ...

HARPAGON.   I'm delighted to share this with you, so that you won't imagine that I said I did have ten thousand crowns in this house. Because I didn't say that, did I!

CLEANTE.   Your affairs are your affairs. Now ...

HARPAGON.   Ah, but if only I did have ten thousand crowns.

CLEANTE.   Father, we wish to ...

HARPAGON.   Think of how easy life would be then.

ELISE.   The reason we're here ...

HARPAGON.   God, how I need those ten thousand crowns!

CLEANTE.   Yes, well ...

HARPAGON.   Then we wouldn't have to complain about how hard times are. Oh, what a mere ten thousand would do!

CLEANTE.   Then just go get it! Everybody knows you can. Everybody knows you have enough.

HARPAGON.   Enough! Do I look like I have enough? Do I act like I have enough? Nothing could be further from the truth and anyone who propagates such a hideous lie should have hat pins stuck in their eyeballs.

ELISE.   Father, your heart.

HARPAGON.   That my own children should become my mortal enemies. Betrayal of the highest degree! Oh, the pain!

CLEANTE. Saying you have money makes me your enemy?
HARPAGON. Yes. Talk like that, not to mention my children strutting about in lace frippery, is bound to lead someone into this very house to cut this very throat in the belief that I might, not that I do, but that I might, have money hidden around here somewhere. Do you want to kill me? It'll be your fault. Between your lies and your extravagant tastes, you'll be the death of me.
CLEANTE. What extravagant tastes?
HARPAGON. Well, let's start with this attire you parade around in, these things you call clothes. Why, what you've got on would be enough to cover my living expenses for a fine retirement. Lace, satin, velvet, gazelle hide, powder, cologne; good lord, you look like Marie Antoinette's boudoir. And smell like her bidet. Where do you get the money for all this?
CLEANTE. Baccarat, my dear father. I gamble, I win, I buy clothes. Someone has to keep up appearances.
HARPAGON. A very bad idea, son, very bad. Save, invest, prepare for a rainy day, for certain as God's wrath, there's going to be one. Armageddon is coming and it's due to fops like you with their ribbons, their bows, and their nasty little hankies. Why I'd bet that the cost of that thing you call a haircut, if invested at eight-point-three-seven-five, compounded quarterly, would within two years bring home easily eighteen livres, six franc four, and twenty groats a year. Now that's appearances! Hoo-eee! *(He sees them exchanging glances.)* What are you doing, planning to jump me and take my money?
ELISE. We're trying to decide who should go first, father. We both have something important to tell you.
HARPAGON. *Quelle coincidence.* I have something to say to you as well.
CLEANTE. It concerns marriage.
HARPAGON. Why yes, yes it does. How did you know that? Tell me, my dear son, you are a fine gentleman, you have a certain *Je ne sais quoi* among the fairer sex; in your travels have you run across a certain woman named Marianne?
CLEANTE. Yes, father.
HARPAGON. *(To Elise.)* And you?

ELISE. I've heard her spoken of.

HARPAGON. And what do you think of this girl, son?

CLEANTE. What do I think of her?

HARPAGON. Why do you repeat my words? Yes, what do you think of her?

CLEANTE. I think she is ... a very charming woman.

HARPAGON. Do you think she's attractive?

CLEANTE. Attractive? Oh, certainly.

HARPAGON. And her manners?

CLEANTE. The *savoir-faire* of a countess.

HARPAGON. Would she not be quite a catch?

CLEANTE. Her husband would be the happiest of men.

HARPAGON. Some housewife, huh?

CLEANTE. The china would sparkle and the cakes would be baked.

HARPAGON. There's only one problem, Cleante. She's broke.

CLEANTE. For heaven's sake, sir; don't let that stand in the way. Money is nothing in comparison with everything else she brings.

HARPAGON. I beg to differ. But perhaps if you could cut back on your expenses, just to oblige your father, there might be some way out of this.

CLEANTE. For her, father, I'll cut to the bone.

HARPAGON. Good boy! So, since we seem to agree, I've made a decision. Provided she can come up with *some* sort of dowry, I have decided, my son, to marry Marianne.

CLEANTE. Huh!

HARPAGON. That's it? Huh?

CLEANTE. *You* have decided ...

HARPAGON. To marry Marianne.

CLEANTE. Who, you, you, you?

HARPAGON. Yes, I, I, I.

CLEANTE. Excuse me father, I have to find a sink. (*Cleante rushes off.*)

HARPAGON. (*Calling after.*) Take two spoonfuls of soda. No, you only need one. (*To himself.*) Sissy. Elise, as for you ... what's wrong with your eyes; they're spinning around like bicycle wheels.

ELISE.   Nothing, father.

HARPAGON.   Where were we? I have decided to marry
Marianne. For your brother I have found a certain rich
widow, and you, Elise, I will give to Seigneur Anselme.

ELISE.   To Seigneur Anselme?

HARPAGON.   Yes, a prudent, wise man, barely fifty. He's
made a fortune in the ivory trade. And you'll inherit everything. Soon.

ELISE.   *(Curtsies.)* I thank you, dearest dada. But I have no
desire to get married, if you please.

HARPAGON.   *(Curtsies back.)* I thank you, dearest pet. But I
should rather you marry him, if you please.

ELISE.   *(Curtsies.)* I beg your pardon, dearest sir.

HARPAGON.   *(Curtsies back.)* I beg your pardon, dearest
madam.

ELISE.   I am Seigneur Anselme's most humble servant, but,
(Curtsies.) with your feelings fully in mind, I shall not marry
him.

HARPAGON.   I am your most humble slave, but, *(Curtsies.)*
with your feelings fully in mind, you shall marry him tonight.

ELISE.   Tonight.

HARPAGON.   Tonight.

ELISE.   *(Curtsies.)* That won't happen, father.

HARPAGON.   *(Curtsies.)* That will happen, daughter.

ELISE.   No.

HARPAGON.   Yes.

ELISE.   No, no, no, no.

HARPAGON.   Yes, yes, yes, yes.

ELISE.   I'll slit my wrists first.

HARPAGON.   I think you won't. I think you will marry him.
Tonight.

ELISE.   Tonight! All the fathers on earth couldn't force me
to do this.

HARPAGON.   My God, why do I have to listen to this?
Don't you know you are my daughter? No sensible person
would object to this match, so why you?

ELISE.   No sensible person would submit themselves to such a mismatch, so why make me?

HARPAGON.   Here comes Valere. He's a sensible young man. We'll let him be the judge.

ELISE.   What a good idea.

HARPAGON.   What he says goes. Deal?

ELISE.   *(Curtsies.)* His word shall be law.

HARPAGON.   *(Curtsies.)* Ironclad, no backing out. *(Valere enters.)* Come here, Valere. You have been appointed judge and jury: which of us is right: myself or my daughter?

VALERE.   Why you, sir, without question.

HARPAGON.   Do you have any idea why we disagree?

VALERE.   No matter, sir. You are the essence of correctness.

HARPAGON.   I intend this very evening to give her a husband, a man as rich as he is erect, and this piece of baggage won't take him. What do you say to that, judge.

VALERE.   *(Fishbone-in-throat-sounds.)* Ngnng ngnng.

HARPAGON.   What?

VALERE.   Ngnng. I say ... I say that I am of your opinion, because you cannot be wrong never. On the other hand, she is not altogether wrong ...

HARPAGON.   What? Seigneur Anselme is the most bountiful catch in the pond: noble, steady, kind, and very well off. He only exploits the best of our colonies. And he's no spring chicken; he won't last that much longer. Could she do better?

VALERE.   No, that's true. But, if she were to speak, which she won't, she might say that she's feeling a bit rushed, just a tiny bit, and perhaps you could give her just a little time ...

HARPAGON.   It's now or never, cookie, got it? He's going to take her — with no dowry.

VALERE.   No dowry!

HARPAGON.   Yes.

VALERE.   Well, case closed. There's no arguing with that, Miss Elise. What a brilliant stroke on your part, sir.

HARPAGON.   I do save a bundle.

VALERE.   No question about that! Still, your daughter might argue, were she to speak, that marriage is, after all, a once in a lifetime proposition, and given a choice between eternal loneliness and eternal agony, she might well prefer ...

HARPAGON.   No dowry!

VALERE.   Absolutely; that shuts your mouth right up. Of course there are people who would tell you of parental love and affection and how they would want to protect their daughter from a dreadful mismatch of age, temperament, and passions.

HARPAGON.   No dowry!

VALERE.   No answering that — that's short, to the point, and absolutely conclusive. Not that there are many fathers that would sacrifice their daughters on the altar of Mammon but who would instead pray for their daughter's bliss, peace, and joy ...

HARPAGON.   No dowry!

VALERE.   Well, that's that. There just is no argument against that. *(The dogs go hysterical in the garden. A bird shrieks.)*

HARPAGON.   *(Aside.)* Oh my God, my strongbox! *(He races out. He comes back in.)* No one leaves this room. *(He races out.)*

ELISE.   What on earth are you doing, Valere?

VALERE.   Looking for a way in. If I go up against him directly, I'll offend him and the game is lost. I throw him a bone, I step back. I lob him a serve, I volley at net. I thrust, I parry, I en garde en pointe ...

ELISE.   This is my marriage we're talking about, Valere!

VALERE.   I know that. Frankly, I don't have a clue what to do.

ELISE.   The clock is ticking.

VALERE.   We've got to buy some time. Pretend you're sick.

ELISE.   What happens when they call in the doctors?

VALERE.   So what; what do they know about it? Write them a check and they'll go away. *(Harpagon re-enters with a mangled bird.)*

HARPAGON.   *(Aside.)* At least I don't have to feed the dogs today.

VALERE.   *(To Elise.)* And if all else fails we'll run away to Morocco and live with the Berbers. Oh Elise, ma belle Elise ... *(He sees Harpagon.)* You must obey your father. Don't look a gift horse in the mouth, especially where "no dowry" is concerned. A good daughter must accept what is given to her.

19

HARPAGON. *(Aside.)* I like this boy. *(To Valere.)* Good words, my son. *(Hands him the bird.)* See what the cook can do with this.

VALERE. Sir, I hope you don't mind me speaking this intimately with your daughter.

HARPAGON. Not at all son. I'm delighted. In fact, I relinquish all my control over her to you. Elise, you are under his power.

VALERE. I'll stay right on her back, sir.

HARPAGON. Yes, by all means.

VALERE. A tight leash, sir.

HARPAGON. Tight and true. Now, I'm going out to have a little stroll. You two be off.

VALERE. *(As they exit.)* Yes, Elise, money is God's highest value. When a man hears "no dowry," God is speaking to him. No selfish prattle from a daughter can stand in the way of prophesy. Here, you take the bird.

HARPAGON. *(Alone.)* He speaks like an oracle! Why couldn't I have had children like that. *(He exits.)*

ACT TWO

Cleante and La Fleche enter, from opposite directions.

CLEANTE.   Well look what the cat dragged in and the dog won't eat! Didn't I give you orders to ...

LA FLECHE.   Yes you did, sir. And there I was, dutifully waiting for you, when out of a corner flies your father, blood in his eyes, foam in his mouth. He searches me, he beats me, he chases me out of the house, and here I am for you, sir.

CLEANTE.   La Fleche, the stakes are now life and death: I've just found out that my father is my rival for Marianne's hand.

LA FLECHE.   Your father in love!?

CLEANTE.   Imagine how I felt when he told me.

LA FLECHE.   Your father in love. If pigs had wings.

CLEANTE.   Well, it seems this one does. We'll need money to fight this war; how goes our loan?

LA FLECHE.   Well sir, you know the phrase "never a borrower or lender be?" That was written by bankers and loan sharks so you'd feel lucky to sign a note with them.

CLEANTE.   Has it fallen through?

LA FLECHE.   Not at all. Our broker, Master Simon, has taken a particular interest in your petition; he says your face alone will serve as collateral.

CLEANTE.   So he can do the full fifteen thousand?

LA FLECHE.   With only a few simple conditions tacked on.

CLEANTE.   And you've been to meet the actual lender?

LA FLECHE.   That's not how the game is played. Borrowing money has more mysteries than the Kabbalah: I couldn't get a hint of who the lender might be. But later today he wants to meet privately with you at the home of a neutral party to learn more about your estate and your family. One mention of your father's name and the deal is done.

CLEANTE.   If I can say it without choking.

LA FLECHE.   Now then, here are just a few clauses the

21

lender dictated to the broker for your approval. *(Pulls out a scroll 12 feet long.) Provided that the borrower be of proper age, family, and estate, free from all encumbrances ...* blah, blah, blah *... bond shall be executed before a notary ... chosen by mutual agreement ...*

CLEANTE.   No problems there.

LA FLECHE.   *The lender, for the benefit of God's eyes and for his own good conscience, will only lend his money at five and one-half percent ...*

CLEANTE.   Five and a half! Well, no objection to that!

LA FLECHE.   *But, conditions being what they are, and the aforesaid lender being obliged to borrow it from someone else at the rate of twenty percent, it is deemed only fair that the aforesaid borrower in turn shall cover this obligation as well.*

CLEANTE.   Wait a minute; who is this thief? That's over twenty-five percent!

LA FLECHE.   Perhaps we should wait for a better deal.

CLEANTE.   How can I? I need the money desperately. My back is at the wall.

LA FLECHE.   That's what I told them.

CLEANTE.   What else?

LA FLECHE.   Oh, nothing really. Odds and ends. *Of the requested fifteen thousand, the aforesaid lender can put down in cash only twelve thousand and therefore the aforesaid borrower will have to take out the remainder in hard goods for which the following addendum be attached.*

CLEANTE.   Hard goods?

LA FLECHE.   *Item: One large yellow and violet canopy bed, lined with satin, Hungary lace, and turkey feathers, very little eaten by the moths, and wanting only one curtain. Item: six stuffed chairs of the same. upholstery only slightly gnawed by squirrel, three frames needing simple repair and joinery, otherwise none the worse for wear.*

CLEANTE.   This is incredible.

LA FLECHE.   *Item: One complete set of well-mended iridescent tapestry depicting the great loves of the ages including: Mars and Venus, he with thunderstalk, she naked, surrounded by raging boars: Adonis and Venus, he with mane of flame, she naked, surrounded by clams and other mollusks; Antony and Cleopatra: he with golden armor and spear, she naked, surrounded by venomous reptiles; and so on through Napoleon and Josephine, she naked; there being eighteen in number, all suitable for bedchamber and guaranteeing great gratification.*

CLEANTE.   Headache. Very bad headache.

LA FLECHE.   *Item: one accompanying set of costumes and props complete with oversize mirror for home re-enactment of above scenes, all in average repair, excepting Caligula and Ivan the Terrible. Item: one lizard skin, stuffed with hay, for hanging from the ceiling complete with hydraulic attachment for spraying jets of liquid from fangs.*

CLEANTE.   That'll be useful.

LA FLECHE.   Just a couple more. *One gold-inlaid game board with variety of delightful games including Jump-On-The-Puppy and Pussy-Eat-Mousey ... etcetera, etcetera, big muskets, empty bottles, silly puppets, giant stone frogs ... the whole of the above certainly worth well over five thousand ...*

CLEANTE.   Over five thousand! I'll never get a hundred for this rubbish. What am I — his trash collector? Twenty-five percent interest plus one ton of garbage. You see what the avarice of a father can drive a son to, La Fleche? And they wonder why we want them dead!

LA FLECHE.   A father such as yours, sir, is enough to make me more than *wish* him dead. For my part, I've always had an aversion to hanging, and I've seen more than one of my companions go a-swinging out of this world; but despite my allergic reaction to the smell of hemp, it'd be a delight to drop the loop over this man's neck and snap it like a chicken bone. Or, if I can't do that, I'd like to rob him of every centime he's got.

CLEANTE.   *(Taking the scroll.)* What else is in here? *(They hear Harpagon's voice and retire. Harpagon enters with Master Simon.)*

MASTER SIMON.   No question, sir. He's a young man, very motivated; he'll sign the contract no matter what contingencies you put on it.

HARPAGON.   But, Simon, what are his resources? What properties are in his estate? Who's his family? What if he defaults?

MASTER SIMON.   I can't give you any particulars, sir; it was only by chance that he was recommended to me. But his servant swears that all is well: his family is quite rich, he is owed a legacy from his mother's death, and it's guaranteed that his father will be cold in the ground within eight months.

HARPAGON.   This all sounds promising. Let's go forward with the loan. "Of faith, hope, charity, the greatest of these is charity." First Corinthians, Simon.

MASTER SIMON.   You won't regret it, sir.

LA FLECHE.   *(To Cleante.)* What the devil is this? That's Master Simon speaking with your father!

CLEANTE.   Someone has spilled the beans. Just who could that be, eh?

MASTER SIMON.   *(To La Fleche.)* Quelle surprise! Who told you that we'd be here? Believe me, sir, I thought our meeting would be in confidence. But no harm; we can come to an understanding right here and now.

HARPAGON.   How?

MASTER SIMON.   *(With Cleante.)* This is the young gentleman who wishes to borrow the fifteen thousand.

HARPAGON.   You! Extravagant fool! Dupe! My own son!

CLEANTE.   You! Shameless usurer! Swine! My own father!
(Simon flees, La Fleche hides.)

HARPAGON.   You would destroy yourself by taking on such interest?

CLEANTE.   You would enrich yourself by lending at such interest?

HARPAGON.   I hope from this moment on that you'll be ashamed to show your face to me.

CLEANTE.   And I hope that you'll be ashamed to show your face to God.

HARPAGON.   After all the toil, sacrifice, and labor I went through for you, this is what I get: excess, deceit, *greed!*

CLEANTE.   You go and ruin the family name by dealing with the lowest of loan sharks, making the house a common hock shop.

HARPAGON.   Out of my sight, scoundrel! Disappear!

CLEANTE.   Just who's the scoundrel: the needy man who borrows what he must or the wealthy man who steals from the needy?

HARPAGON. I said go. Go, go, go! *(Alone.)* Well, that helped pass the time. And it gives me an excuse to watch his comings and goings ever more closely. *(The dogs erupt. Frosine enters from the garden, tugging at her dress which she finally frees from the jaws of the Dobermans.)*

FROSINE. Monsieur Harpagon, comment ca va?

HARPAGON. Wait here! Right here. There. Don't move! *(He races into the garden.)*

LA FLECHE. *(To himself.)* He must have a regular furniture store hidden somewhere. I don't recognize anything mentioned in the contract.

FROSINE. Well, look who's here as I live and breathe!

LA FLECHE. Frosine, Frosine, Frosine! What on earth brings you here?

FROSINE. Oh, the usual — a little this, a little that, some fetching, some carrying; making myself useful with whatever small talents God gave to me. Its a hard world out there, Fleshy, and only wit and cunning will get you through.

LA FLECHE. Something for the master, then?

FROSINE. I fix for him, he gives to me a small reward.

LA FLECHE. He does, huh?

FROSINE. Ah, La Fleche, ma fleche, men have been known to go without food and shelter for the commodities I trade in. There are certain services for which any man will pay dearly.

LA FLECHE. I beg your pardon, but the word "man" implies that this person is somehow related to the human race, a bad assumption, Frosine. And "pay" is not a word he knows; he won't even pay you his respects; he'll only lend them to you. With interest.

FROSINE. My God, Fleshy, you underestimate me. Why, I know all one needs to know about men: where to stroke them, how to arouse them, where their soft spots lie.

LA FLECHE. There are no soft spots to be touched on this one, my love; he'd rather tear out his vitals than give up a sous. As for arousal, perhaps if this body of yours changed into gold, there might be some small reaction, but failing that.... Here he comes; here I go. *(Exits.)*

HARPAGON. *(Aside.)* Everything's safe. *(Aloud.)* So, Frosine,
How is our little business coming along?
FROSINE. My, my, my. If you aren't the picture of health.
HARPAGON. Who, me?
FROSINE. I've never seen you with such a glowing complex-
ion.
HARPAGON. Really.
FROSINE. So fresh, so pert. I've seen twenty-five-year olds
who look older than you.
HARPAGON. Nonetheless, Frosine, I am over sixty.
FROSINE. Sixty! The prime of manhood.
HARPAGON. Well, actually I wouldn't mind trading back
about twenty years.
FROSINE. Non, non, non, non. No need of that. You have
the stuff to live to be a hundred.
HARPAGON. Think so?
FROSINE. You show all the signs. Look into the light; yes,
there it is: right between your eyes, the mark of long life.
HARPAGON. You know about these things?
FROSINE. But of course. Give me your hand. Mon Dieu,
what a life-line. Forget a hundred! I see easily one-twenty, one-
thirty.
HARPAGON. That's twice my age now.
FROSINE. You'll live to bury your children's children.
HARPAGON. That'll be a relief. But meanwhile, how is our
little business?
FROSINE. Need you ask? There are many things I can
make, Monsieur Harpagon, but match-making is what I do
best of all. In our case I have spoken intimately with both our
ladies about you. I told poor, sick mama that you had fallen
head over heels for Marianne from the moment you peered
through her window.
HARPAGON. And mama said...?
FROSINE. She was ecstatic! Then she had a coughing fit.
And then I told her that you would like Marianne to be
present tonight when you sign your own daughter's marriage
warrant. She agreed without hesitation and put Marianne in
my charge.

HARPAGON. I'm obliged to give a supper for Monsieur Anselme tonight; what better time for Marianne to meet the family. And me.

FROSINE. Perfect timing.

HARPAGON. I'll send my coach to pick her up.

FROSINE. Ideal.

HARPAGON. But, Frosine, you did remind the mother that this is a marriage and therefore a dowry is expected? After all, no one, no matter how much in love, is going to marry a girl who doesn't bring a little something to the bargain.

FROSINE. A little something! This is a girl who guarantees you twelve thousand francs, *per annum!*

HARPAGON. Twelve thousand!

FROSINE. *Per annum.* First off, she   slip of a thing, used to a diet of apples, bread crust, and weak tea. No pate de foie gras, no crêpe flambé, no Armagnac for this one, not like other married women. Why this alone will save you three thousand francs. Then, there's her taste for the simple life: no gowns, no pearls, no Louis Quartorze furnishings — no, no, no; the barest necessities are enough to please our Marianne, saving you minimum four thousand francs. *Per annum.* And, last but not least, she is morally repulsed by gambling, which, as you know, is a common fixation with married ladies these days; why I know of one wife who drops more than twenty thousand *per annum* at roulette, but let's take only a quarter of that. Five thousand a year at the gaming table, four thousand in clothes, jewelry, and furnishing, there's nine which added to your three for food totals twelve thousand francs. For you. *Per annum.*

HARPAGON. Not bad, not bad. But it adds up to nothing tangible.

FROSINE. Pardonnez-moi. Nothing tangible to bring you sparse diet, simple taste, and a fervent rejection of gambling?

HARPAGON. Tangible, my dear lady: something I can hold onto. I can't bank a dowry made of expenses she won't spend.

FROSINE. You'll be holding on to plenty; they've spoken to me of some foreign land where they own counties of property

— it'll be yours, all yours.

HARPAGON.   We'll see about that. But Frosine, there's another thing: while she's no child, still she's young and the young generally fall in love only with their equals. To be frank, I worry that a man my age might not, well, attract her, and this could lead to, how to put it, marital ... discord.

FROSINE.   Aha, are you in luck! Young men completely nauseate her and she is an absolute fool for older men.

HARPAGON.   Marianne is?

FROSINE.   Our Marianne. You should hear her on the subject: the spite she has for callow boys. But oh how she waxes poetic over older men: their beards, their little folds of gristle, the hair in their nostrils; there is no part of an older man that does not excite her. The older the better, so I warn you when you meet her look older than you are; anything below sixty and you've had it. In fact, four months ago she broke off an engagement when her paramour boasted that he was fifty-six and did not put on his spectacles to read the marriage warrant.

HARPAGON.   Just for that?

FROSINE.   Just for that. You should see what the sight of a bespectacled nose does to her.

HARPAGON.   *(He puts on his eyeglasses.)* You know, if I had been a woman I never would have cared for young men either.

FROSINE.   I would hope not. A bunch of fops, a parade of dandies; they're the intangible ones: absolutely nothing you can hold in your hand.

HARPAGON.   What kind of woman could see something in that?

FROSINE.   Not a real woman. Can you imagine loving such a preening popinjay?

HARPAGON.   You know I say that every day: I hate their nasty chicken-squeak voices, their scraggly little chin hairs, their perfumes that smell like swamp gas, and those hairless little bosoms popping out of those unbuttoned shirts.

FROSINE.   And compare that to you! This is the way a *man* looks. See, see, see! I'd better sit; I'm not sure I can take too much more of this.

HARPAGON.   Do I ... arouse you?

FROSINE.   Arouse isn't the word; I can't even say the word in polite company. Turn around, turn around slowly; oh, I wish I could paint you, sculpt you in marble, capture this essence of masculine power. Keep turning; oh I'm feeling faint.

HARPAGON.   *(Still turning.)* I am pretty healthy; just a little mucus now and then. *(He coughs into a hankie.)*

FROSINE.   Oh, but you bear it so gracefully. Walk. I like to watch from behind.

HARPAGON.   *(As he walks.)* Tell me, has Marianne seen me yet, peering through her window?

FROSINE.   No, but we've talked a lot about you — oh, the hips, the hips — and I've sung your praises to the skies, told her how lucky she'd be to have such a husband. Little does she know.

HARPAGON.   You've done well, Frosine. Thank you.

FROSINE.   I have just a slight request I'd like to make, sir. *(He stops.)* I'm in a little legal scrape, nothing really, but I'm afraid that I might lose the case because all my funds are tied up right now, so I wondered if ... *(He is frowning.)* Marianne's eyes sparkled like diamonds when I talked about you, and you should have heard the little involuntary cooing that came from her throat, like pigeons. *(He smiles.)* To tell the truth, this lawsuit is a bit more serious than I just let on; indeed if I lose, I'm ruined, devastated really. Just a little assistance would be ... *(He is frowning.)* And then her ruby lips erupted into human cries, then animal shrieks of ecstasy as she called out your name: Harpagon! Harpagon! In short, sir, I've made her extremely anxious to get this wedding concluded.

HARPAGON.   Frosine, I'm delighted. I can't tell you how much I'm obliged to you .

FROSINE.   Well then, all I need is a little bit. Just to see me through this troubled time.

HARPAGON.   Good-bye. I have a supper to plan.

FROSINE.   Sir, I can't tell you how urgent this is.

HARPAGON.   Go fetch Marianne; bring her here for introductions, then you, she, and my stupid little daughter shall go off to the carnival 'til supper time. Bye now, and don't go out through the garden when you leave.

FROSINE. *(Kneeling.)* Oh my God, sir. Please have mercy. *(Prostrate.)* I'll die if you don't help. Save me, save me!

HARPAGON. Where's that wind coming from? I'd better shut the windows. A bientot, Frosine. *(He exits.)*

FROSINE. Go rot in hell, you withered prune with your dried up little acorns. Damn, no one has ever held out on me like this; I'm on the floor, for God's sake! Get up, woman, get up. *(She does.)* We're far from done, Monsieur Harpagon. I have not yet begun to fight. *(Music plays, dogs howl, and light changes.)*

ACT THREE

Enter Harpagon, Cleante, Elise, Valere, La Fleche and Master Jacques.

HARPAGON. All right everybody: here are your orders. You, La Fleche, take this broom and clean up everything. Everything. When you're done take this rag and rub off the furniture, but not too hard or you'll break it. And during the supper you'll be in charge of bottles and glasses, but I warn you if one thing ends up missing, you'll pay for it ten times over.

MASTER JACQUES. *(Aside.)* A smart move.

HARPAGON. After you wash the glasses — carefully — you will be in charge of serving the drinks, but only to people who are truly in need. This is not some Champs-Elysee restaurant; no fawning, no forcing them to drink, no standing around with a stupid grin on your face and a towel on your sleeve. Start with water, and only when they ask several times should you pour.

MASTER JACQUES. *(Aside.)* Oh, this'll be a merry little fete.

HARPAGON. As for you Elise, my budgie, see that not a morsel of food, not a giblet, is thrown out. We'll save what's left for the dogs when we decide to feed them. Meanwhile, doll up for my fiancée; You can certainly look better than this.

ELISE. Yes, father. *(She exits.)*

HARPAGON. *(To Cleante.)* As for you, poodle eyes, I've been good enough to forgive your recent transgressions, so no gloomy-face from you in front of my bride-to-be.

CLEANTE. I Father? How could you ...

HARPAGON. Everyone knows how children feel when their father re-marries, especially to a beautiful young thing. So keep your hands to yourself and a smile on the face, fop. Disinheritance is only a pen stroke away.

CLEANTE. I can't promise you I'll be happy to have her as a stepmother, father. But I will obey your wishes and welcome her to the house.

HARPAGON. Remember, you're on very thin ice. (*Cleante and La Fleche exit.*) Now, Valere, I'll need your help on this. Master Jacques, approach.

MASTER JACQUES. Excuse me sir, but whom do you wish to speak to: your cook or your coachman?

HARPAGON. Both.

MASTER JACQUES. Which one first, sir.

HARPAGON. The cook.

MASTER JACQUES. Moment, s'il vous plait, sir. (*He takes off his livery coat and appears in a chef's outfit.*) Now then.

HARPAGON. I have promised, Master Jacques, a grand supper tonight.

MASTER JACQUES. A grand supper! Marvelous!

HARPAGON. And I'm counting on you to come up with something special.

MASTER JACQUES. No problem, sir, if you give me plenty of money.

HARPAGON. Money, always money! Don't you people know any other word? Money, money, money; morning, noon, and night! Haven't you got something better to do with your mouth than say the word "money" all the time.

VALERE. (*To Jacques.*) Where's your imagination? Any fool can put on a grand meal with plenty of money, but the true chef knows how to put on a feast with next to nothing.

MASTER JACQUES. A great meal with no money!

VALERE. Yes.

MASTER JACQUES. Well perhaps, Mr. Maitre D', you will show us exactly how to do that by taking my place as cook (*Puts the hat on Valere's head.*) since you love meddling in every one else's business so much. Go stir your ladle, lackey.

HARPAGON. Silence. What provisions will we need?

MASTER JACQUES. Ask Mr. Cordon Bleu here since he knows about making something out of nothing.

HARPAGON. I want an answer from *you! Now!*

MASTER JACQUES. How many people at table?

HARPAGON.   Eight or ten. But assume eight. If there are ten, there will more than enough food.

MASTER JACQUES.   Excellent. We will start with escargot, tripe, truffle, snout, squab, and sweetmeats, with Dom Perignon '27 as a palate washer. Then the bouillon course ...

HARPAGON.   Wait a minute, we're not feeding the entire fourth arrondisement.

MASTER JACQUES.   Deer sinew soup with calf bollocks, artichoke puree with aorta of bunny heart ...

HARPAGON.   Hold it!

MASTER JACQUES.   And the meats: tender tips of ox gland, roast ...

HARPAGON.   *(Clapping his hand over Jacques' mouth.)* Stop! You'll eat me out of house and home.

MASTER JACQUES.   Side-dishes ...

VALERE.   Do you think we're inviting people over to bloat them to death? No doctor in his right mind would let anyone eat all this. Of the seven deadly sins, gluttony is surely the most life-threatening.

HARPAGON.   This is a very smart man, Master Jacques. You pay attention.

VALERE.   Wretched excess, Mr. Jacques, this is wretched excess. We are not, after all, swine at the trough. This is a refined dinner we're preparing, a light repast, a concerto for the taste buds, not an assault on the esophagus. As the wise man said: "We must eat to live, not live to eat."

HARPAGON.   Listen to that. Come here, I want to hug you for that. This is the finest sentence I have ever heard in my life: "We must live to eat, not ... " No, that's not it. What was it, again?

VALERE.   "We must eat to live, not live to eat."

HARPAGON.   That's it, that's it! Do you hear that, Jacques: "We must ... " Who was it said this?

VALERE.   I don't remember just now.

HARPAGON.   Write those words down for me, will you? I want them engraved in gold on the dining-room mantle.

VALERE.   I'll see to it, sir. Meanwhile, as for supper, leave it to me. I'll take care of everything.

HARPAGON. You're in charge, son.

VALERE. My pleasure, sir.

HARPAGON. We need nice, cheap, fatty, things so that people will be done soon and won't ask for more. How about head cheese with beans?

VALERE. Sounds perfect, sir.

HARPAGON. And you, Master Jacques, go clean the coach.

MASTER JACQUES. Wait; that's a matter for the coachman. *(Puts his livery coat on.)* Now then, you were saying...?

HARPAGON. Air out the carriage, curry the horses, and prepare to fetch my fiancée. You're taking her, Frosine, and my stupid little daughter to the carnival 'til supper time.

MASTER JACQUES. The horses? Have you seen the poor beasts lately? You kept them on such a fast that they can barely stand, much less drag a carriage. These aren't horses, but shadows shaped like horses.

HARPAGON. How can they be ill; they don't do anything.

MASTER JACQUES. And for that they should starve? Do you know how it hurts me to see them like this? It breaks my heart, it does, because I feel exactly like them. I *know* their suffering; why every day I pull my measly rations right out of my mouth and feed it to them. The animals are our friends, sir; we must not let them famish.

HARPAGON. I imagine they can make it from here to my fiancée's house; I know I can.

MASTER JACQUES. No, sir; I haven't the heart to drive them. One crack of the whip and thud: glue factory.

VALERE. I'll handle it, sir. Our neighbor will be happy to team them and drive the women to the carnival.

MASTER JACQUES. Good. At least I won't have two dead horses to answer for.

VALERE. Well, look who's suddenly getting a conscience.

MASTER JACQUES. Well, look who's suddenly getting indispensable.

HARPAGON. Enough!

MASTER JACQUES. Pardon me, sir, but I despise flatterers, and this paysan is one of the first order. Horning in everywhere, looking after the bread, the wine, the salt, the milk —

34

he does this with only one purpose, sir: to flatter you. It makes people talk about you, sir, and that makes me so mad I could scream, sir, because, after my horses, I love you most of all.

HARPAGON.   These people who talk, Master Jacques — what exactly do they say?

MASTER JACQUES.   Oh, I can't, sir. You'll get angry.

HARPAGON.   No, please.

MASTER JACQUES.   You'll only go into a rage and that would upset me.

HARPAGON.   Not at all, far from it. Like any other man, I'd love to know what the world thinks of me. You'll be doing me a favor.

MASTER JACQUES.   Well, since you insist, I'll be frank: you are the butt of a thousand jokes, all about how mean you are. For instance, they say that you keep a special almanac in which the fast days of all the religions of the world are marked down, so that you won't have to feed us on holy days. They say that you spend the entire month of December picking fights with footmen, doormen, and other servants so that you won't have to give them a Christmas bonus. They say that you tried to sue the neighbor's cat for lapping up some cream from our kitchen. They say you save your mouthwash to use again. In short, sir, you are the laughing-stock of all Paris. They use words like stingy, tightwad, codger, lick penny, harpy, extortioner, usurer, venal, covetous — things like that.

HARPAGON.   *(After a long neutral silence.)* Valere, beat the crap out of him. *(Harpagon takes Master Jacques' livery whip, hands it to Valere, and exits.)*

VALERE.   So, "lackey," we see what your truth-telling gets you.

MASTER JACQUES.   Stick to your own business, milquetoast. This is no affair of yours.

VALERE.   Oh, now he's threatening me.

MASTER JACQUES.   *(Aside.)* He's knuckling under, I can tell. Two quick moves and I'll have him screaming for mercy. *(To Valere.)* Laugh all you want, sonny, but soon you'll be laughing through puffy lips. *(He charges Valere forcing him across stage.)*

VALERE. Take it easy.

MASTER JACQUES. Ha! Easy. He wants me to take it easy.

VALERE. Please ...

MASTER JACQUES. Give me the whip, toady, and I'll show you easy.

VALERE. *(Brandishing whip.)* Give you the whip; my pleasure.

MASTER JACQUES. Hey, wait a minute. I didn't mean that.

VALERE. Are you aware, scullery rat, of the power I have over you?

MASTER JACQUES. I get it, I get it.

VALERE. And that you are nothing but a pot scrubber, a horse feeder.

MASTER JACQUES. Pot scrubber, horse feeder.

VALERE. And that you don't have a clue who you're speaking to when you call me lackey.

MASTER JACQUES. I take it back. Not a lackey, not a lackey.

VALERE. *You* will whip *me*, you say?

MASTER JACQUES. Only kidding! Hah! Jokes, jokes!

VALERE. Not funny. Your jokes are not funny. *(He cracks the whip several times in Jacques' direction.)* Hah! Hah! Hah! Now *that's* funny. *(Deeply satisfied, Valere tosses down the whip and leaves.)*

MASTER JACQUES. *(Alone.)* So much for honesty. Never again. From now on, I just lie, that's all there is to it. *(With the whip.)* From my master maybe I take a whipping, but not from this puppy. He'll hear from me again; vengeance is mine. Die. Die. Die. *(As he cracks the whip on a chaise, Marianne and Frosine enter. Marianne screams.)*

FROSINE. Nothing to worry about, Marianne. Hello, Jacques. Is your master at home?

MASTER JACQUES. Given the way things are going, I'd say he is.

FROSINE. Why don't you run along and get him. *(Jacques exits.)*

MARIANNE. This is going to be horrible.

FROSINE. Why? What is there to worry about?

MARIANNE.   What would you worry about if your neck was directly under the guillotine?

FROSINE.   I know. I can see that marrying Harpagon must seem like a terrible death sentence; and if I guess correctly, your heart is still fixed on that handsome young man who came calling.

MARIANNE.   Why deny it. He was gentle, kind; a bit over-dressed, but nice.

FROSINE.   And did you find out who he is?

MARIANNE.   We didn't get that far. I remember the vein just below his earlobe. I wanted to lick it.

FROSINE.   Marianne, you need to get out more. There's more to life than a whiff of musk and a fine line of talk. Charmers like that are all over Paris, moussing their hair, rouging their cheeks, and not one franc to their name. What you need is a mature husband, one that can lay a good settlement on you. Sure, you'll have your fits of depression, maybe even a little hospitalization, but soon he'll be dead, you'll be rich, and that'll make up for everything.

MARIANNE.   What a dreadful idea, waiting for someone to die so that I can be happy.

FROSINE.   Think of your poor mother.

MARIANNE.   Death doesn't always fit it with our plans. I've learned that lesson.

FROSINE.   That can be taken care of: you marry Harpagon only on the strict condition that he makes you a widow *post haste*. Say six months — no, three. Get it in the contract. Anything else would be less than fair — oh, but here he comes. Big smile.

MARIANNE.   O God, Frosine, look at that face! (*Enter Harpagon, followed by Valere.*)

HARPAGON.   Don't be offended, mon petit bon-bon, that I come to meet you with my spectacles on. I know that your earthly charms are radiant enough to dazzle the naked eye, but it is through lenses that we observe the stars, you know, and you yourself are the brightest light of the firmament, nay, a galaxy of delights to the soul and to this delicate, but oh so passionate, frame. (*A deadly stillness.*) Frosine, why isn't she saying anything?

FROSINE.   She's a bit overcome, monsieur. You know how bashful young girls are.

HARPAGON.   Hmm. Perhaps you're right. *(To Marianne.)* Well, this'll cheer you up sweetie. Here comes my little daughter Elise to welcome you. She has flowers from our garden. *(Elise hands Marianne a bundle of dead weeds.)*

ELISE.   It's the best I could do.

MARIANNE.   Please forgive me for not paying my respects earlier.

ELISE.   Au contraire, I should have come to visit you.

HARPAGON.   See what a tubby one she's getting to be, Marianne? But ill weeds grow fast, huh, tender tips? *(Kisses Marianne's fingers.)*

MARIANNE.   *(To Frosine.)* What a hideous man.

HARPAGON.   What says my honey-love?

FROSINE.   She was saying how you leave her speechless.

MARIANNE.   *(To Frosine.)* He's worse than my worst nightmares.

HARPAGON.   No need to be shy.

MARIANNE.   *(To Frosine.)* I've got to get out of here. *(As she attempts to flee, she sees Cleante.)* Oh!

HARPAGON.   And here comes my son to welcome you to our house.

MARIANNE.   *(To Frosine.)* Frosine, it's him.

FROSINE.   *(To Marianne.)* Who?

MARIANNE.   *(To Frosine.)* Ear lobe, ear lobe!

FROSINE.   Well, isn't this fun!

HARPAGON.   I see you're surprised by my grown-up children; don't worry they'll be out of our hair in no time at all.

CLEANTE.   Madame, permit me to say how taken aback I am by these unforeseen circumstances. It was only today that my father told me of his intentions.

MARIANNE.   I am as surprised as you, monsieur. I was ... not prepared for this meeting.

CLEANTE.   My father has chosen well, madame; indeed, he could not do better and I am delighted to meet you. But my excitement does not extend to the design you may have of becoming my step-mother, the last title I would wish upon you. Harsh as this may sound to some, I hope that you will take my meaning in the proper spirit: the thought of these nuptials, sadly, repels me, clashing, as they do with my own interests. In brief, were it left to me, with the generous permission of my father, this marriage would not take place.

HARPAGON. What kind of idiotic greeting is this?

MARIANNE. And sir, in reply I vow unto you that things are equal on my side; if you are offended by seeing me as your step-mother, I am no less offended at the thought of you as my step-son. Please, don't think that it is I who seek to cause you pain and misery; unless I were compelled to it by higher powers than myself, I swear to you that I would not consent to a marriage that could cause you even the slightest unhappiness.

HARPAGON. Well put. To an idiotic greeting, an appropriate response. My dear, forgive him his little, youthful indiscretions. Don't be upset; he's a babbling twit who knows not what he says.

MARIANNE. I'm not the least upset; indeed I find his candor quite refreshing. Anything less than total frankness, and I would only think the less of him.

HARPAGON. You're too generous. But perhaps time will age him, and he'll see the folly of his ways.

CLEANTE. No, father, as a matter of fact I won't change my mind on this point. I beg the lady to believe me.

HARPAGON. You're piling it on, son. Just drop it.

CLEANTE. And go against the wishes of my heart?

HARPAGON. Change the subject, Cleante. It's over. *(Slaps him.)*

CLEANTE. Right. Since my father wishes for me to speak in a different way, allow me, madame, to put myself in his shoes and confess that I have seen nothing in this world so beautiful as you; I can conceive no higher purpose in God's eyes than pleasing you; and that to become your husband would be a destiny I would prefer to ruling the greatest kingdoms on this globe. There is nothing I would shrink from to make so precious a conquest. I would vanquish any adversary, annihilate any opponent ...

HARPAGON. You're a little overboard, son. Slow down.

CLEANTE. But sir, these compliments I pay the young madame are from you.

HARPAGON. Good God, you think I can't do it myself.

FROSINE. How about the young ones and I all go to the carnival now; that way we're back sooner with more time to continue this merry banter.

HARPAGON. Valere, see that the horses are teamed up. Oh, but I forgot, dainty duck; would you like some refreshments before you leave? Valere, chairs all around and rummage about for something to eat.

CLEANTE. I've taken care of it father. I've ordered Mandarin oranges, Tahitian kiwi, and Tasmanian cumquat — it's all on your tab.

HARPAGON. *(Softly.)* Valere!

VALERE. He's lost his marbles, sir.

CLEANTE. Are you worried that's not enough? My lady will perhaps forgive any deficiency on my part.

MARIANNE. You needn't have bothered.

HARPAGON. *(Covers Cleante mouth.)* That's enough out of you.

CLEANTE. *(Grabs Harpagon's hand.)* Madame, have you ever seen a diamond that sparkles as much as the one on my father's finger?

MARIANNE. It certainly does shine.

CLEANTE. *(Having slipped the ring off.)* Look at it up close.

MARIANNE. It sends beams around the room — beautiful.

CLEANTE. No, madame, it is in your hands that it is beautiful. My father gives it to you.

HARPAGON. He does!

CLEANTE. An expression of his love.

HARPAGON. *(Aside.)* What are you doing?

CLEANTE. *(Aside.)* What kind of question is that? *(Aloud.)* He asks you to put it on.

MARIANNE. I ... can't. *(She offers it back.)*

CLEANTE. No, no, no. He wants you to keep it.

HARPAGON. *(Aside.)* I'm going to rip his eyeballs out!

MARIANNE. *(Offers again.)* But I ...

CLEANTE. No, you mustn't refuse. You'll only offend him.

MARIANNE. I beg you.

CLEANTE. Nothing I can do.

HARPAGON. *(Aside.)* Feed his lungs to the dogs.

CLEANTE. See how angry he's getting because you won't take it?

HARPAGON. *(Aside.)* I spit in his mother's milk. Toof! Toof! Toof!

CLEANTE. You're really upsetting him.

HARPAGON. *(Writhing and clutching his heart.)* You're killing me.

CLEANTE. It's not my fault, father. I'm doing everything I can to make her keep it.

HARPAGON. *(To Cleante.)* I going to die and come back and plague you.

CLEANTE. Mademoiselle, he's threatening me; you see what you're doing?

HARPAGON. *(Exorcist devil voice.)* You'll have my blood on your hands.

CLEANTE. I'm very worried about him, mademoiselle. Please take the ring.

FROSINE. Good Lord, keep the thing. Peace at any price.

MARIANNE. *(Crosses to Harpagon who is gagging on the floor.)* I'll keep it for now, if you want me to, sir, but I'll give it back at some more convenient moment. *(Harpagon looks at her with great, teary love and attempts to kiss her. She flees as La Fleche enters.)*

LA FLECHE. Sir, there's a man wishes to speak to you.

HARPAGON. Tell him I'm busy.

LA FLECHE. He says he has some money for you.

HARPAGON. Beg your pardon, Marianne; I'll be right back. *(Master Jacques enters, slamming violently into the exiting Harpagon.)*

MASTER JACQUES. Sir ...

HARPAGON. I am slain!

VALERE. Sir, are you all right?

HARPAGON. My creditors put him up to this. Murder! Police!

MASTER JACQUES.   Sorry, sir; I thought you'd want the news.

HARPAGON.   What news?

MASTER JACQUES.   Both of the horses have lost their shoes.

HARPAGON.   Take them to the blacksmith. La Fleche don't let the man at the door get away! *(Jacques and La Fleche exit.)*

CLEANTE.   In the meanwhile father, I'll entertain our guests out in the garden. Valere, fetch the fruit! *(All are out before Harpagon can protest; the dogs are howling. Music, wind, thunder.)*

HARPAGON.   Oh my God, my God, my God, they're in the garden. Cleante, I curse the day you were born. But we're not done yet, son of mine; and when I'm through with you, we'll see who destroys who. *(Intermission.)*

ACT FOUR

Rain is beginning to fall; an occasional drop plops to the floor. Cleante sticks his head in from the garden.

CLEANTE.   The coast is clear. We can get out of the rain now. *(Marianne, Elise, and Frosine follow Cleante into the room.)*

ELISE.   *(To Marianne.)* My brother's told me everything; I know his affections for you are real; I also know the agony of forbidden love, believe me I know, and I'll do anything I can to help.

MARIANNE.   I'm so grateful to have made a friend like you; I know I'm going to need one.

FROSINE.   *(To Marianne.)* Why the hell didn't you tell me about this? Had I known, I wouldn't have pushed things so far with Mister Personality.

CLEANTE.   It's all my fault. My stars shine darkly over us and I have doomed us to this fate. Marianne, what can we do?

MARIANNE.   I'm at the will of my mother; it's her dying wish that I marry a wealthy older man. Thanks to you, Frosine, that wish has been realized, contract and all. What else can we do but hope for the best?

CLEANTE.   That'll go a long way. Is there nothing more you can offer me? A little pity, a little solace, your lap to rest my head in?

MARIANNE.   I have nothing but pity; but how can I go against the wishes of my mother who sacrificed everything for me? You talk to her, see if you can change her mind.

CLEANTE.   She hates me; I knew it from the first day she saw me.

MARIANNE.   She did find you repulsive.

CLEANTE.   Frosine, you're the only chance we've got; you come up with something. I know you can.

MARIANNE.   Yes, you, Frosine.

ELISE.   You got them into this.

FROSINE.   Easier said than done, children. *(To Marianne.)*

Turning your mother around isn't out of the question, she's a decent woman. Besides, she's old and not that tightly wrapped — her we could win over. *(To Cleante.)* The real problem, the way I read the cards, is your father.

CLEANTE.   Always has been.

FROSINE.   Break the contract and he'll howl like a banshee. It's out of the question that he'd let you sprint home with the trophy he so desperately sought. No use getting mama to reject him. We have to figure out some way for him to reject Marianne.

CLEANTE.   Now there's a thought!

FROSINE.   Give me a moment here, something's coming. *(She looks heavenward.)* Wait! What's the one thing he loves more than Marianne?

CLEANTE and MARIANNE.   Money!

ELISE.   The Dobermans!

FROSINE.   Money. Let's just say we could come up with someone, a very wealthy someone, for instance, someone his own age with slag heaps of money and a title or two to boot — we'll say the Baroness of Lower Bougainvillea for now — and let's say that your father just happened to find out that she was head over heels for him and was willing to place a hundred thousand crowns on the table, plus a few chateaux, a railroad or two, all this just for the right to marry him. What happens then?

ALL.   He dumps Marianne and marries her.

CLEANTE.   But there's no baroness like that; this'll never work.

FROSINE.   Leave the Baroness to me. You, Cleante, figure out some way to pay me for all this.

CLEANTE.   You have my assurances. Marianne, turn those bountiful charms that have so slain my heart on to your mother; she must let you out of your side of the contract. Beg, cajole, bring up childhood memories, sing sad songs, quack like a duck — whatever it takes — just convince her. And then, we are each others to caress 'til death do us part. *(He kisses her hand. She strokes his earlobe.)*

HARPAGON.   *(Aside, unseen by the others.)* Well, well, well;

what mysteries have we here? The stepson kissing the step-
mother who seems to not mind in the slightest.

ELISE. *(Very loud.)* Bonjour, Papa!

HARPAGON. *(Coldly.)* The carriage is ready. Go to the carnival. Have a good time. Not you, Cleante. *(All but Cleante de-
part.)* Well now, let's just pretend she wasn't your stepmother
— what do you think of her.

CLEANTE. Her?

HARPAGON. Her.

CLEANTE. Marianne. What do I think of her.

HARPAGON. Say, for instance, her looks, her intelligence,
her fingers.

CLEANTE. Comme ci, comme ca.

HARPAGON. That's it?

CLEANTE. Well, to speak candidly, she's not what I expected. She's a flirt, that's all, not even a very pretty flirt. Not
that bright either. But please, do what you will father. She's
as good as any other stepmother, I suppose.

HARPAGON. But just a moment ago I heard ...

CLEANTE. Some sappy words. Greeting card platitudes. Just
to please you.

HARPAGON. So she arouses no interest on your part whatsoever.

CLEANTE. Interest? None at all.

HARPAGON. I'm sorry to hear that. You see, as I was standing there I began to reflect on my age and the obvious dif-
ference between me and Marianne and I began to realize that
it could cause quite a scandal, she and I. People would talk.
So I began to think I would give up on this silly little notion
and turn her over to you. Had not you taken a dislike to her.

CLEANTE. To me?... you would have ...

HARPAGON. Yes, to you.

CLEANTE. In marriage?

HARPAGON. In marriage.

CLEANTE. Well, she isn't exactly my idea of a good time,
but to please you, father ...

HARPAGON. No, no, no. I'd never force anything on you.

CLEANTE. But, you see, for your sake, I'd make any effort.

HARPAGON.   Son, there's nothing worse than a loveless marriage. I wouldn't do that to you.

CLEANTE.   But perhaps we'd grow on one another, father; they say that love is often the fruit that wedlock bears.

HARPAGON.   Bad poets and women say that, my son. The truth is harsher: infidelity, alcoholism, fatal accidents — these are the realities; you wouldn't want that, would you, son? Had you had any inclinations toward her, that would be different; I'd be proud to lead you to the altar. But, that not being the case, I'll go back to my original plan and marry her myself.

CLEANTE.   I'll come clean, father: I love her, love her very much, and have since the first day I saw her. I planned to propose marriage to her and have been looking for the right time to seek your permission.

HARPAGON.   Have you been going to her house?

CLEANTE.   Yes, father.

HARPAGON.   Frequently?

CLEANTE.   Enough, given how short a time I've known her.

HARPAGON.   And you've been welcomed?

CLEANTE.   Very much so, but without her knowing who I really was; that's why she panicked when she saw me here.

HARPAGON.   And you've told her you love her and want to marry her?

CLEANTE.   Yes; and I've discussed it with her mother as well.

HARPAGON.   And her mother was receptive?

CLEANTE.   She listened very carefully and kindly.

HARPAGON.   And the daughter returns your affections.

CLEANTE.   If I don't flatter myself, father, I do believe she has some affection for me.

HARPAGON.   So, now we know. Son, do you know what you will have to do? Forget about her. She's mine, not yours, mine. You will marry the rich widow I spoke of earlier and that's that. In your mind, Marianne no longer exists. Repeat after me: Marianne no longer exists.

CLEANTE.   So that's the game you're playing: I bare my soul so you can catch me in your trap! Well, it won't work; I'll never give up Marianne and I'll stop at nothing to make sure that you can't get near her. You may have a contract with her mother's signature, but I have other weapons (*Pulls his earlobes.*), and believe me, I'll use them.

HARPAGON.   Poacher! Stay out of my hunting grounds.

CLEANTE.   I got there first.

HARPAGON.   I am your father, young man. You owe me!

CLEANTE.   Where love is concerned I owe you nothing!

HARPAGON.   I'll beat your brains to vichyssoise.

CLEANTE.   Don't flatter yourself, old man.

HARPAGON.   Repeat after me: Marianne does not exist!

CLEANTE.   My father does not exist! (*Harpagon rushes to a corner and grabs a pike out a suit of armor. He chases Cleante down the hall. While they are offstage, the armor, with a big steak in its back hand, walks out the garden doors into the rain. The dogs bark wildly, the armor flings the meat towards them, they go quiet. The armor moves towards the dogs. Harpagon chases Cleante back into the room. Master Jacques comes tearing in from the other direction.*)

MASTER JACQUES.   Good God, what is *this!* Gentlemen, gentlemen!

HARPAGON.   (*To Cleante.*) My son does not exist!

CLEANTE.   My father does not exist!

MASTER JACQUES.   (*To Cleante.*) Come, sir, gently.

HARPAGON.   Let me at him.

MASTER JACQUES.   Sir, sir. You would do this to your son?

HARPAGON.   Yes!

MASTER JACQUES.   To me, maybe, but to your own flesh and blood?

HARPAGON.   Master Jacques, I command you to mediate this dispute, to prove that I am in the right.

MASTER JACQUES.   Whatever it takes. You stand there, and you — there. (*Rain is dripping through the ceiling by now; Jacques distributes umbrellas and goes to Harpagon.*) Now, sir.

HARPAGON.   I am smitten with a woman whom I wish to marry and lover boy there has moved in on her.

MASTER JACQUES.   He is wrong to do that.

HARPAGON.   He owes me the respect to bugger off and leave her to me.

MASTER JACQUES.   Dead right! You wait here and I'll go

speak to him. *(Crosses to Cleante.)* Now, sir, what have got to say for yourself?

CLEANTE.   I've fallen madly in love with a lovely woman, my own age; my father gets wind of it and proposes to her himself.

MASTER JACQUES.   He is wrong to do that.

CLEANTE.   At his age. He ought to be ashamed of himself and leave love to the young. He's had his chances.

MASTER JACQUES.   You are dead right. He's only kidding around. Stay here and I'll go talk with him. *(With Harpagon.)* A very reasonable young man, your son. He sends his respects to you and begs you to realize that he was only carried away by a fit of passion. He is more than willing to step aside provided you treat him better and allow him to choose a wife that he finds attractive.

HARPAGON.   Since he looks at it that way, tell him Master Jacques, that he can look forward to parental love and affection from me. He can choose anyone he wants for a wife, with the exception of Marianne.

MASTER JACQUES.   I'll see what I can do. *(With Cleante.)* The savage beast is soothed; he says it was only your temper that upset him and that he would be more than happy to let you have whatever you want, anything at all, as long as you show him the respect a son owes a father.

CLEANTE.   Master Jacques, assure him I shall honor and obey his every wish, as long as he grants me Marianne.

MASTER JACQUES.   *(With Harpagon.)* Done. He's agreed to everything.

HARPAGON.   Bless him.

MASTER JACQUES.   *(With Cleante.)* Done. He sends his blessings.

CLEANTE.   Praise God.

MASTER JACQUES.   Gentleman, I declare this little contretemps over. May peace reign forever and ever.

CLEANTE.   Master Jacques, you are a man among men.

MASTER JACQUES.   Don't mention it, sir.

HARPAGON.   Master Jacques, you have my eternal gratitude; this deserves a reward. *(Jacques looks expectantly.)* Run along; I'll remember this when the time comes. *(Jacques shrugs and exits as thunder claps.)*

CLEANTE.   Father, I beg your forgiveness. I'm afraid I went a bit out of control. It happens; it's been a problem for me.

HARPAGON.   Forget it, son.

CLEANTE.   I bathe in the river of regret father. I wash away my sins.

HARPAGON.   Yes; I can see that. And it makes me glad, son.

CLEANTE.   *(Kissing Harpagon's hand.)* How good of you to forgive me so quickly.

HARPAGON.   One's children are easy to forgive, Cleante, especially when they remember their duty to their parents.

CLEANTE.   And you don't harbor any resentment at all for my ... behavior? It was a bit much.

HARPAGON.   None whatsoever, son; I see you have repented and begun anew.

CLEANTE.   I shall carry the radiance of your charity to my grave, sir. It shall illuminate my darkness.

HARPAGON.   And for my part, son, I shall delight in beneficence; name it and it shall be yours.

CLEANTE.   Oh no really, father; what more could I want now that you've given me Marianne.

HARPAGON.   Excuse me?

CLEANTE.   I was saying that by giving me Marianne, you've given me more than I could ever wish for.

HARPAGON.   Who said anything about giving you Marianne?

CLEANTE.   You did, father.

HARPAGON.   I did!

CLEANTE.   Absolutely.

HARPAGON.   No, no, no. What happened is that you promised to forget about her.

CLEANTE.   Me? Forget about her?

HARPAGON.   Yes.

CLEANTE.   Not a chance.

HARPAGON.   There's not a chance that you'll forget about her?

CLEANTE.   I'm more determined than ever to marry her.

HARPAGON.   Double-dealer! Traitor!

CLEANTE.   Nothing will change my mind.

HARPAGON.   You are forbidden from my sight.

CLEANTE.   Fine.

HARPAGON.   I abandon you.

CLEANTE.   Great.

HARPAGON.   I disown you.

CLEANTE.   Terrific.

HARPAGON.   ˉ I dis-in-her-it you. *(Throws Cleante into the orchestra seats.)* And when you die, I spit my curses on your coffin. *(Exits.)*

CLEANTE.   *(Calling after.)* Thank you, sir. That's very generous of you. *(Huge lightning flash and thunder crack; the dogs howl, the garden doors fly open, wind flies through the house. The suit of armor totters in carrying a muddy strongbox. Seeing this, Cleante drops to his knees.)* Our father, who art in heaven ...

THE SUIT OF ARMOR.   Get up, Cleante.

CLEANTE.   Yes, sir.

THE SUIT OF ARMOR.   *(Handing him the muddy strongbox.)* Take this.

CLEANTE.   My clothes ...

THE SUIT OF ARMOR   We'll get them cleaned.

CLEANTE.   *(With box.)* Who are you and what's in here?

THE SUIT OF ARMOR.   Your father's treasure: ten thousand crowns, pure gold. *(Raises visor.)* I figured out where it was and waited for the right moment.

CLEANTE.   La Fleche! You look ridiculous.

LA FLECHE.   And how would you get around those mutts? *(Outside, the mutts start barking; Harpagon howls.)* We've got to get out of here. *(They flee the best they can, Cleante pushing the strongbox down the hall, La Fleche wobbling after. Lightning, thunder, the wind is at peak. Through the garden door flies Harpagon.)*

HARPAGON.   Thieves! Thieves! Assassins! Murderers! In the name of justice, stop the murderers! Oh my God, I'm done for, they've cut my throat, they've murdered me, they have stolen my money! All right, come out; I know you're in here! Who is he? Where is he hiding? How can I find him? Which way should I run? Which way should I not run? Who's there?

There he is! Get him! *(He attacks his own throat, wrestling it to the floor.)* Stop thief; murderer; give me my money back! Who are you; speak up! ... Oh, it's me. I'm falling apart. Who am I? Harpagon. Where am I? My house. What's going on? *(Cries.)* Oh my money, my dearest, darling money, my beloved — where have you gone? They've taken you from me. I've lost everything, my foundation, my joy, my consolation — I can't live without you, without you life has no purpose, without you I am nothing; nothing, nothing, nothing. Now I am dying. Now I am dead. Now I am buried. Now there is nothing. *(Silence. He is supine. Then he whispers:)* Is there any one out there who would like to revive me by telling me where my money is? Or at least who took it? Ssst, what do you say — anyone? You? You? No one? I hear nothing — nothing, nothing, nothing. Pull yourself together, Harpagon: get on the case. Justice must reign. Inform the authorities, cross-examine the entire household — female servants, male servants, son, daughter, dogs, myself — Lord, what a disgusting crowd. And I suspect the whole lot of them. Every last one of them is guilty, guilty, guilty — what the hell was that? What are you talking about back there? *(He lays a plank from the stage to the audience.)* What's that whispering about? What's the commotion back there? Have you got the thief? Is the thief back there with you? *(He is wading over the audience seats now.)* For God's sake, if you know anything about the thief, tell me. I'll pay you handsomely — *(He picks up a woman's purse.)* — anything you want! *(He takes a man's wristwatch.)* Anything at all. *(Looks at the watch.)* We can do a lot better than this! Tell me where he is! They're all looking at me. And laughing, right in my face. Hah, hah, hah. You'll see, they're all in it, up to their necks; guilty, guilty, all of them: guilty! *(He returns to the stage, pulling a bell cord.)* Hurry! Everybody hurry! Police, sheriffs, bailiffs, magistrates, judges, supreme court justices, gallows attendants, executioners — I want the whole world hanged, all of them, everybody, hanged! And if I don't get my money back, then I will hang myself. *(He wraps the bell cord around his neck and pulls it up and down with his body. The bells, the storm, the dogs, and a long-suffering female soloist climax and fade.)*

ACT FIVE

Enter Harpagon and the Chief of Police.

CHIEF OF POLICE. Leave it to me; I know my job. This isn't the first robbery I've been involved in. If I had a hundred francs for every robber I've hung, I'd be a rich man today.

HARPAGON. How rich?

CHIEF OF POLICE. Very rich.

HARPAGON. I'll make you even richer. But if you don't find my money, I'll see that you hang.

CHIEF OF POLICE. Right. Why don't we begin at the beginning. There was this box ...

HARPAGON. With ten thousand crowns in it.

CHIEF OF POLICE. Ten thousand crowns!

HARPAGON. Cash. Pure gold.

CHIEF OF POLICE. This is quite a heist!

HARPAGON. And the punishment should fit the crime. Before the hanging there should be torture: cuticle extraction, ground glass omelet, acid enemas. Then the hanging. Otherwise there is nothing sacred in the world.

CHIEF OF POLICE. Um-hmm. And who are your suspects?

HARPAGON. Every one. These people. First arrest them. Then everybody in those stores over there, spending money. My money. Then the suburbs.

CHIEF OF POLICE. Why don't we start a little closer to home; we don't want to frighten anybody and lose our advantage. How about we collect a little evidence first and then spring it on them, snap, like a mousetrap.

MASTER JACQUES. *(Enters calling down the hall.)* String him up by the feet, cut his throat and drain it. Then drop him in the boiling oil 'til his skin is nice and crispy. Then we'll eat him.

HARPAGON. You've found the thief!

MASTER JACQUES. Well, no sir. I'm talking to that uppity

steward of yours, sir: Valere. About the pig we're preparing for dinner.

HARPAGON. You're sure? *(Jacques nods.)* Well, this man needs to speak to you. *(Jacques startles at the uniform.)*

CHIEF OF POLICE. Don't worry — I'm not going to cause you any harm. Now as we have our little chat, I want you to remember your duty to your master; you must tell him everything you know.

MASTER JACQUES. I know my cooking, sir. I'd be glad to tell him everything I know about the pig. *(Heads towards kitchen.)*

HARPAGON. That won't be necessary.

MASTER JACQUES. Of course, like anything, if we had a little more money — why this very pig could be spiced and marinated ...

HARPAGON. We're not talking about the pig! Who stole my money!

MASTER JACQUES. Someone stole your money?

HARPAGON. Yes someone stole my money and I'll hang you like a squealing pig if you don't give it back. Now!

CHIEF OF POLICE. Now, now; have a care. This is clearly an honest man; one look at his face and you can see just how honest he is: he'll tell you everything you need to know, no threats necessary. What eyes — so innocent. Now, all you have to do is confess and no harm will come to you. As a matter of fact your master will give you a substantial reward. So tell us what you know about this little affair. I'm sure you know something.

MASTER JACQUES. *(Aside.)* Now's my chance to repay the little sniveling steward.

HARPAGON. What are you muttering about, piglet?

CHIEF OF POLICE. Easy, easy. He's working up to a confession. I told you he was an honest man.

MASTER JACQUES. Sir, it causes me untold agony to say this, and I know how much more it will hurt you, but it was your steward who did this.

HARPAGON. Valere!

MASTER JACQUES. Valere. The steward.

HARPAGON. He! who seemed so loyal, so upright ...

MASTER JACQUES. I'm deeply sorry, sir.

HARPAGON. And what is your proof?

MASTER JACQUES. Proof?

HARPAGON. Proof. Evidence.

MASTER JACQUES. It is true ... because I believe it.

CHIEF OF POLICE. We'll have to do a little better than that, lamb.

HARPAGON. Have you seen him hanging around the place where I had my money hidden?

MASTER JACQUES. Hanging around? Absolutely sir. Where was your money hidden?

HARPAGON. In the garden.

MASTER JACQUES. Yes, that's just where I've seen him hanging around. In the garden. And what was your money in again?

HARPAGON. A strongbox.

MASTER JACQUES. That's what I saw him with. A strongbox.

HARPAGON. What kind of strongbox.

MASTER JACQUES. What kind?

HARPAGON. Yes, what kind?

MASTER JACQUES. Well, it was like a strong box.

CHIEF OF POLICE. Perhaps a detail or two.

MASTER JACQUES. Big — it's a big box.

HARPAGON. Mine was small.

MASTER JACQUES. Big in terms of what it had in it. Small box, big inside.

CHIEF OF POLICE. What color?

MASTER JACQUES. The color. You want to know the color?

CHIEF OF POLICE. Yes.

MASTER JACQUES. Well, I'd say ... Let's all try to remember.

HARPAGON. You go ahead.

MASTER JACQUES. It was red, right?

HARPAGON. No, gray.

MASTER JACQUES. That's it. A sort of slate-red. You might even call it gray, depending on the light. A gray strongbox, not very large, but lots in it.

HARPAGON. That's mine! No question about it. Swear out the warrant, chief. My God, my God, my God — from now on I trust no one, myself included.

MASTER JACQUES. This is him, now, sir. Please don't tell him I'm the one who indicted him. *(Valere enters.)*

HARPAGON. Valere. Down. Kneel. Lower. Now confess to the most heinous crime ever committed by mankind ever.

VALERE. What are you talking about, sir?

HARPAGON. Aha! No remorse, no contrition. The mind and soul of a hardened criminal.

VALERE. What crime are you talking about?

HARPAGON. What crime! Monster; as if you didn't know. Go ahead, cheat, lie, prevaricate — you'll only twist in the wind longer. How could you take advantage of my feelings for you, the trust I placed in you? I loved you, Valere. And then you go and pull off the dirtiest, cruelest trick ever perpetrated by man.

VALERE. Sir, my honor forbids me to lie. I deny nothing.

MASTER JACQUES. *(Aside.)* Zut alors, I'm a prophet!

VALERE. It is my fault for not speaking to you earlier, sir. I've been waiting for the right opportunity. I've failed you; I see that. But I beg of you a chance to explain my reasons.

HARPAGON. Reasons, hah! Thief. Swindler. Fraud.

VALERE. These are all names I deserve, sir. And more. But perhaps when you hear the other side of the story you will find more affectionate terms.

HARPAGON. What other side of the story can there be? You have murdered me, Valere, driven a white-hot knife through the fragile tissue of my aged heart.

VALERE. That which your heart so dearly loves, sir, has not fallen into bad hands. I am of rank and status to care for it providentially; there's nothing here that can't be fixed.

HARPAGON. Then fix it. You owe me, toad — give me back what's mine. As pure and clean as when I left it.

VALERE. Your honor shall be satisfied, sir.

HARPAGON. Honor, schmonor. Who put you up to this vicious assault?

VALERE.   Need you ask?

HARPAGON.   Yes, I need ask. What scoundrel drove you into this?

VALERE.   A god on high who makes all men dumb as a post. Love.

HARPAGON.   Love?

VALERE.   Yes.

HARPAGON.   Love for my money. Gold-digger!

VALERE.   No sir, your wealth had nothing to do with it. I ask for nothing more than what I've already taken.

HARPAGON.   No! You can't have it. It's mine, mine, mine. Get this: he robs me of the dearest thing to my heart and now he wants to keep it!

VALERE.   I wouldn't call it robbery, sir.

HARPAGON.   Oh you wouldn't! A treasure like that. Why else would I keep it locked and hidden from everyone else?

VALERE.   I agree, it is a treasure well worth keeping under lock and key. But you wouldn't be losing it if you gave it to me. I beg you on my knees, sir, let me keep the treasure box whose lock I have picked; you will never regret it, sir.

HARPAGON.   What are you talking about?

VALERE.   We have pledged our faith to each other, your treasure and I, and sworn never to part.

HARPAGON.   That I wish I'd seen.

VALERE.   We have vowed to be all things to each other, forever.

HARPAGON.   Don't count your chickens, little man.

VALERE.   'Til death do us part.

HARPAGON.   He's got gold fever.

VALERE.   And whatever motives you may ascribe to me, I can assure that I acted only from the purest of intentions.

HARPAGON.   A Christian saint, right here in our midst. Where's the cat-o-nine tails?

VALERE.   I am willing to suffer whatever consequences you may inflict. But I beg you to believe that I alone am to be blamed; your daughter played no part in this.

HARPAGON.   My daughter — I would certainly hope not. Let's quit pussyfooting around; where have you taken the love of my life?

VALERE.   Taken, sir? Nowhere. Your treasure is still in the house.

HARPAGON.   *(Aside.)* Oh! My little box, still in the house. *(To Valere.)* You've not damaged my treasure, have you? Rummaged around in it? Rubbed it with your stubby little fingers?

VALERE.   Sir! My love burns with a pure and holy flame.

HARPAGON.   *(Aside.)* He burns for my strongbox!

VALERE.   I would sooner die than dishonor her.

HARPAGON.   Dishonor? My strongbox?

VALERE.   I admit I have enjoyed the sight of her, sir — oh how my eyes gazed over her golden lobes, her twinkling orbs — but nothing could tempt me to sully her innocent beauty.

HARPAGON.   Golden lobes? Twinkling orbs? This fellow's further gone than I thought.

VALERE.   The scullery maid knows the truth, sir; she can testify.

HARPAGON.   What! The scullery maid is an accomplice to the crime? Write that down, chief.

VALERE.   She was witness, sir, to our passion and to our pledge of eternal fidelity.

HARPAGON.   *(Aside.)* I'm really pretty worried about him.

VALERE.   And, sir, I assure you again, your daughter's chastity remains intact.

HARPAGON.   My daughter's what?

VALERE.   She has made me vow, in a written promise of marriage, sworn before the scullery maid, that we shall forestall the consummation of our passion until the night of our nuptials.

HARPAGON.   You're going to have nuptials with my daughter?

VALERE.   Yes, sir. Nuptials.

HARPAGON.   Larceny, nuptials — my life is a train wreck! Chief, throw the book at him — a hundred counts of theft and child molestation.

MASTER JACQUES.   Make that two hundred.

VALERE.   These charges are unjust! Wait 'til you find out exactly who I — *(Enter laden with soggy carnival detritus: Elise,*

Marianne, Frosine.)
HARPAGON.   You wretched, ungrateful hussy of a daughter, conniving trollop; is this how you thank me: taking up with a thief, scudding about in the scullery, having nuptials without my consent! Oh, how you two will pay. *(To Elise.)* For you, a dark pit with vermin and slugs; and for you *(To Valere.)* the gallows at sunset.
VALERE.   I refuse to be condemned by a raving madman. I demand a fair trial.
HARPAGON.   But first we'll rip your sinews on the rack.
ELISE.   Oh father, I beg your mercy — please don't let parental passion push you to an act you will regret. Take the time to consider, for, sir, as you have often said to me: all that glitters is not gold. So the reverse can be said as well — take another look at Valere; he is not what you think him to be. And once you know the truth, as now only God does, you will see why I have given myself to him. It was fated that he and I should meet, that it be he who would save me from the surging undertow that threatened to engulf me that day at the shore; it is he to whom you owe the very existence of your loving daughter ...
HARPAGON.   I wish you both had drowned.
ELISE.   Father, with all the love of a daughter to her father, I beg you ...
HARPAGON.   Love of a father! Groping about under the stairs and stealing my money — where's the love in that? Chief, get on with it — Let justice be swift and harsh.
MASTER JACQUES.   And so the worm has turned, Master Valere.
FROSINE.   This is much more fun than that dreadful carnival. *(Anselme enters, bedecked in velvet and ivory.)*
ANSELME.   My dear Harpagon! You're not looking so good — are you all right?
HARPAGON.   Ah, Monsieur Anselme, I'm afraid your marriage contract is in jeopardy. And me — before you see a man besieged: my honor, my property, my very soul all attacked by this thief of love who has insinuated himself into my house as a servant to pillage my property and

prestidigitate the purity of my progeny.

VALERE.   Who cares about your money!

HARPAGON.   They've gone and got engaged, Monsieur Anselme — a direct insult to you and I urge you to press charges on this profligate for alienation of affection and loss of services. Revenge is the only course a man can take.

ANSELME.   Far be it for me to force a marriage on an unwilling partner and lay claim on optioned property; but where your interests are concerned, sir, you can rely on me to uphold them as if they were my own.

HARPAGON.   And here you see, sir, an honest magistrate, ready and willing to enforce the law to the letter. Chief, do your duty for God and the Republic — take him away and show no mercy.

VALERE.   What crime can it be to love your daughter? When you find out who I am —

HARPAGON.   Who cares who you are! This town's full of impostors, poseurs, masqueraders; say what you will, to me you're nothing but a lackey.

MASTER JACQUES.   That's my noble master!

VALERE.   Be not so free with your words, sir. By birth and by privilege I have right to this fair maid. Anyone in Naples can testify to my rank.

ANSELME.   Naples. Your dart has hit the wrong spot on the globe, young man. You're speaking in front of a man to whom all Naples is known and who can see right through your little tale. You might want to throw again.

VALERE.   If you know Napoli, sir, then you know Don Tomas D'Albruzzi.

ANSELME.   Few people know him better than I.

HARPAGON.   Don Tomas, Don Giovanni — enough of these operas.

ANSELME.   No, no — let him speak. His words alone may hang him. What of this D'Albruzzi?

VALERE.   He was my father.

ANSELME.   Don Tomas D'Albruzzi was your father! Come, come you can do better than that.

VALERE.   There is nothing better than that. My father was

the noblest of Neapolitan nobles.

ANSELME.   But you, young man, are mistaken. Don Tomas D'Albruzzi, his wife, and children were lost in a storm at sea sixteen years ago following the great purge which exiled the highest nobles of the town.

VALERE.   Ah, but there's more, sir. His seven year old son was saved from the shipwreck and taken aboard a Spanish frigate and raised up as the captain's own son. I am that boy; educated at Barcelona in the military arts. Recently word reached me that my father too had survived the shipwreck. I set across Europe in search of him and in the course of my travels fate sent me to the beach where I found Elise in the undertow. I rescued her, became a slave to her charms, and temporarily suspended my search so that I might make her my wife.

ANSELME.   An amusing tale, well concocted. But it lacks credibility, young man; anyone could have made this up.

VALERE.   For proof I offer this agate bracelet which my mother, God rest her soul, wore on her arm as the ship capsized.

MARIANNE.   Could I see that? *(She holds up an identical bracelet.)* Brother?

VALERE.   Sister?

MARIANNE.   Brother!

VALERE.   Sister!

MARIANNE.   I knew it, I knew it, I knew it; the moment you opened your mouth, I knew it. A thousand times my mother has told me the same horrible story, the shipwreck, the screaming children, then she cries. I remember we were captured by pirates, some had only empty sockets where their eyes should have been, but the food was good. I think that's right. Anyway, somehow we got to Naples, or was it Genoa; which one has the funny building that's falling over? No, no — I mean the stinky rivers for streets; is that Florence? I don't think we were ever in America. I don't have any money. So you're my brother? You don't look that much like me. Well, here we are in Paris, only I never go outside because mother has rickets, but I'm sure she'll be glad to see you anyway. She just can't dance very well. Do you have any money?

ANSELME. *(Holds up a third bracelet.)* Children!

VALERE. Father?

MARIANNE. Father?

ANSELME. Children!

VALERE. Father!

MARIANNE. Father! *(They embrace.)* Do you have any money?

ANSELME. Yes, my daughter, yes, my son; I am Don Tomas D'Albruzzi, whom heaven saved from the waves and swept to the shores of Africa on the back of a mast. It's a strange place, Africa; one doesn't get much sleep: bugs, drumming, general unrest. But a diligent man can do well — cheap labor, wildlife on the hoof, it all adds up. But I missed, well, you might say civilization, though they wouldn't see it that way. I leave that argument to my betters. The siren call of the city cried out; restaurants, parks, women younger than I. Naples was out; one purge in a lifetime is enough. And due to some little, well, business misunderstandings back on the dark continent, I decided to change my name as well. So, here I am in Paris: Count Anselme.

HARPAGON. Is this your son?

ANSELME. Yes.

HARPAGON. Then I hold you accountable for the ten thousand crowns of which he has robbed me.

ANSELME. He? Robbed you?

HARPAGON. He robbed me.

VALERE. Just who told you this?

HARPAGON. Master Jacques.

MASTER JACQUES. I? Said that?

HARPAGON. It's in the book, Jacques. He wrote it down.

VALERE. And do you really believe I'd do such a thing?

HARPAGON. Belief has nothing to do with it. I just want my money back. *(Enter Cleante and La Fleche.)*

CLEANTE. Have no fear, father; this can be arranged. Here's the bargain: I give you your money, you give me Marianne.

HARPAGON. You know where it is?

CLEANTE. It's in a nice safe place. Which is it — your

strongbox or Marianne?

HARPAGON.   Has anything been removed?

CLEANTE.   Not a sous. Her mother has agreed to leave the decision to Marianne; she marries whomever she wants, provided of course you free her from the contract.

MARIANNE.   Except, Cleante, it's not that easy. There's also my father and my brother to contend with.

ANSELME.   God has not re-united me with my children so that I might contradict their wishes. Marianne, you are free to choose.

MARIANNE.   Me? I've never made a decision in my life.

ANSELME.   Monsieur Harpagon, you are well aware what decision she will make, once she comes around to it. Consent to this double betrothal, as I do.

HARPAGON.   Before I consent, I have to see my strongbox.

CLEANTE.   In good time, sir — safe and sound.

HARPAGON.   There's not a centime in there for my children, marriage or no. I don't have any money. For them.

ANSELME.   Well, I have money for them.

HARPAGON.   And you'll pay for these weddings?

ANSELME.   Rehearsal, reception and all.

HARPAGON.   I'll need a new suit.

ANSELME.   Done. Jacques, champagne — I'm paying. Let us rejoice in the happiness of the day.

CHIEF OF POLICE.   Hello, hello. Just who's going to pay for my time here. Police work doesn't come cheap.

HARPAGON.   *(Pointing to Master Jacques.)* There, there's your payment. Take him and hang him.

MASTER JACQUES.   What's a poor man to do? First I'm beaten for telling the truth and now I'm to be hung for lying!

ANSELME.   Now, now Monsieur Harpagon; on a day like today surely we can find a way to forgive his little white lies.

HARPAGON.   You'll pay off the chief then?

ANSELME.   Happily. But first let us dance, and dance, and dance. Then we will surprise your mother and share our joy with her. Perhaps even she will dance. *(Music.)*

HARPAGON.   *(Cutting off music.)* No dance! Not until I see my strongbox! (*Cleante orders La Fleche to bring it to Harpagon. All dance to a rousing song by the long-suffering soloist as Harpagon lies on the floor fondling his strongbox. Fade to black.*)

END

PROPERTY LIST

ON-STAGE PRESET
The central playing space is kept as bare as possible (three dust-covered chairs were strewn about in the original production and moved as needed) with price-tagged objects piled into the corners of the set. The effect is that of a yard sale in a crumbling townhouse. In the on-stage clutter sit the following practical props:

CENTER
> Three covered Louis XIV chairs

PERIMETER
> Armor with pike (substituted by LA FLECHE in
> identical armor during post-intermission blackout)
> 3 ravaged umbrellas (closed) for JACQUES
> 1 large plank for HARPAGON to bridge to audience
> Bell cord for HARPAGON to pull
> Buckets to catch rain
> Folding screen (for JACQUES cook/coachman quick
>   changes)

OFF STAGE LEFT TABLE
> Mangled pigeon (HARPAGON)
> Livery whip (JACQUES)
> Bouquet of weeds (ELISE)
> Diamond ring (worn) (HARPAGON)
> Strongbox (muddy) (LA FLECHE)
> Shovel (muddy) (HARPAGON)

OFF STAGE RIGHT TABLE
> Scroll (LA FLECHE)
> Contract/Pen (MASTER SIMON)
> Steak (for dogs in armor bit) (LA FLECHE)
> Notebook/Pen (CHIEF OF POLICE)

Carnival detritus (soggy) (ELISE, MARIANNE, FROSINE)
Money — lots of it (ANSELME)

PERSONAL
Eyeglasses (HARPAGON)
Handkerchief(s) (CLEANTE)
Agate bracelets (1 each) (VALERE, MARIANNE, ANSELME)

COSTUME PLOT

Note: The costumes in the original production of this translation were based on flamboyant early 19th-century French fashions (even though the set reflected a time some 40 years later; c'est la guerre). Particularly useful in costuming was a Cruikshank caricature entitled "Monstrosities of 1827."

VALERE
>   Tattered waistcoat
>   Old vest
>   Plain shirt with tie
>   Simple breeches
>   Boots
>   Keys

ELISE
>   Elegant dress (on-stage practical)
>   Bustle and undergarments
>   Brocade stockings
>   Slipper shoes
>   Bows, earrings, etc.

CLEANTE
>   Swallowtail coat (garish)
>   Ruffle and vest
>   Tight pants
>   High-buckle shoes
>   Rings, hankies, etc.

HARPAGON
>   Formerly elegant black cape w/unraveled gold piping
>   Smudgy undershirt
>   Soup-stained vest
>   Baggy knickers, worn at knees, fastened by large pins
>   Ragged stockings

Old slippers
Head turbans

LA FLECHE

Hat (conceals stolen objects)
Ragged coat with many pockets
Balloon pants tied with rope
Soft-soled boots

MASTER SIMON

Crumpled top hat
Long coat
Vest and shirt
Blousy old pants
Various faux chains and fobs — cheap and garish
Shoes

FROSINE

Over-sequined tight-fit red dress, generally dazzling
Net stockings
Ridiculous hat

MASTER JACQUES

Cook's hat, quite beaten
Apron
Ragged shirt and vest
Non-descript pants
Coachman's Hat
Livery Coat (on-stage practical)

MARIANNE

Nice but simple dress; soft fabrics, pink and blue
Stupid hat
Purse festooned with fruit
Dainty slippers

CHIEF OF POLICE
>Gendarme officer's outfit with braid and medallions galore
>High boots

ANSELME
>Top hat of oiled jaguar fur
>Incredibly elegant longcoat (forest green with ivory trim)
>High-neck white scarf wrap with stickpin
>Gold chain and medallion
>Ebony walking stick with gold and ivory trim

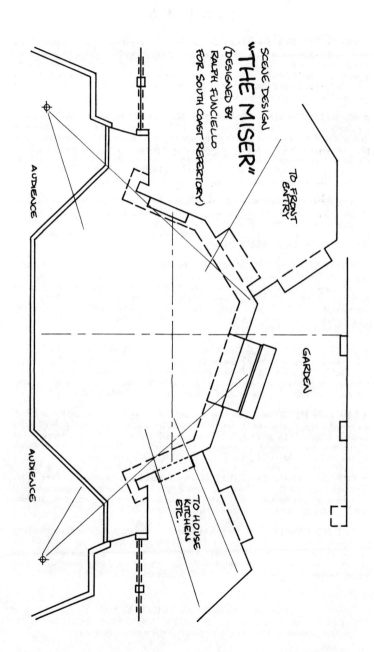

SCENE DESIGN
"THE MISER"
(DESIGNED BY
RALPH FUNCIELLO
FOR SOUTH COAST REPERTORY)

TO FRONT ENTRY

AUDIENCE

AUDIENCE

GARDEN

TO HOUSE KITCHEN ETC.

NEW PLAYS

★ **SHEL'S SHORTS by Shel Silverstein.** Lauded poet, songwriter and author of children's books, the incomparable Shel Silverstein's short plays are deeply infused with the same wicked sense of humor that made him famous. "…[a] childlike honesty and twisted sense of humor." *–Boston Herald*. "…terse dialogue and an absurdity laced with a tang of dread give [*Shel's Shorts*] more than a trace of Samuel Beckett's comic existentialism." *–Boston Phoenix*. [flexible casting] ISBN: 0-8222-1897-6

★ **AN ADULT EVENING OF SHEL SILVERSTEIN by Shel Silverstein.** Welcome to the darkly comic world of Shel Silverstein, a world where nothing is as it seems and where the most innocent conversation can turn menacing in an instant. These ten imaginative plays vary widely in content, but the style is unmistakable. "…[*An Adult Evening*] shows off Silverstein's virtuosic gift for wordplay…[and] sends the audience out…with a clear appreciation of human nature as perverse and laughable." *–NY Times*. [flexible casting] ISBN: 0-8222-1873-9

★ **WHERE'S MY MONEY? by John Patrick Shanley.** A caustic and sardonic vivisection of the institution of marriage, laced with the author's inimitable razor-sharp wit. "…Shanley's gift for acid-laced one-liners and emotionally tumescent exchanges is certainly potent…" *–Variety*. "…lively, smart, occasionally scary and rich in reverse wisdom." *–NY Times*. [3M, 3W] ISBN: 0-8222-1865-8

★ **A FEW STOUT INDIVIDUALS by John Guare.** A wonderfully screwy comedy-drama that figures Ulysses S. Grant in the throes of writing his memoirs, surrounded by a cast of fantastical characters, including the Emperor and Empress of Japan, the opera star Adelina Patti and Mark Twain. "Guare's smarts, passion and creativity skyrocket to awesome heights…" *–Star Ledger*. "…precisely the kind of good new play that you might call an everyday miracle…every minute of it is fresh and newly alive…" *–Village Voice*. [10M, 3W] ISBN: 0-8222-1907-7

★ **BREATH, BOOM by Kia Corthron.** A look at fourteen years in the life of Prix, a Bronx native, from her ruthless girl-gang leadership at sixteen through her coming to maturity at thirty. "…vivid world, believable and eye-opening, a place worthy of a dramatic visit, where no one would want to live but many have to." *–NY Times*. "…rich with humor, terse vernacular strength and gritty detail…" *–Variety*. [1M, 9W] ISBN: 0-8222-1849-6

★ **THE LATE HENRY MOSS by Sam Shepard.** Two antagonistic brothers, Ray and Earl, are brought together after their father, Henry Moss, is found dead in his seedy New Mexico home in this classic Shepard tale. "…His singular gift has been for building mysteries out of the ordinary ingredients of American family life…" *–NY Times*. "…rich moments …Shepard finds gold." *–LA Times*. [7M, 1W] ISBN: 0-8222-1858-5

★ **THE CARPETBAGGER'S CHILDREN by Horton Foote.** One family's history spanning from the Civil War to WWII is evocatively intertwining recounted by three sisters in monologues. "…bittersweet music—[a] rhapsody of ambivalence…in its modest, garrulous way…theatrically daring." *–The New Yorker*. [3W] ISBN: 0-8222-1843-7

★ **THE NINA VARIATIONS by Steven Dietz.** In this funny, fierce and heartbreaking homage to *The Seagull*, Dietz puts Chekhov's star-crossed lovers in a room and doesn't let them out. "A perfect little jewel of a play…" *–Shepherdstown Chronicle*. "…a delightful revelation of a writer at play; and also an odd, haunting, moving theater piece of lingering beauty." *–Eastside Journal (Seattle)*. [1M, 1W (flexible casting)] ISBN: 0-8222-1891-7

DRAMATISTS PLAY SERVICE, INC.
440 Park Avenue South, New York, NY 10016   212-683-8960   Fax 212-213-1539
postmaster@dramatists.com   www.dramatists.com